The
Early Greek
Concept of
the Soul

*Published for the Center
for Hellenic Studies*

THE
EARLY GREEK
CONCEPT OF
THE SOUL

Jan Bremmer

PRINCETON UNIVERSITY PRESS

Published by Princeton University Press, 41 William Street,
Princeton, New Jersey 08540
In the United Kingdom: Princeton University Press,
Chichester, West Sussex

LIBRARY OF CONGRESS CATALOGING-IN-PUBLICATION DATA
Bremmer, Jan N.
The early Greek concept of the soul.

"Published for the Center for Hellenic Studies."
Bibliography: p.
Includes index.
1. Soul—History of doctrines.   2. Greece—Religion.   I. Title.
BL795.S62B73   1983   128′.1   83-18627
ISBN 0-691-03131-2
ISBN 0-691-10190-6 (pbk.)

First Princeton Paperback printing, 1987
Fourth printing, for the Mythos series, 1993

Princeton University Press books are printed on acid-free paper
and meet the guidelines for permanence and durability of the
Committee on Production Guidelines for Book Longevity of the
Council on Library Resources

10   9   8   7   6   5   4

Printed in the United States of America

To My Parents

Contents

Acknowledgments

THIS BOOK developed from a thesis defended at the Free University of Amsterdam in 1979, and it is with deep gratitude that I thank Professor G.J.D. Aalders for his able and pleasant supervision of my work and Professor D. M. Schenkeveld, who acted as co-referent, for his valuable criticism. I also owe special thanks to Professor Walter Burkert of Zürich for his early interest in this study, his many comments, and, above all, for the inspiration his work has been—and still is—for my own interest in Greek religion.

I am especially indebted to those friends and colleagues who read and criticized the entire manuscript or parts of it: Richard Buxton, who in addition corrected the English of the dissertation, John Gould, Fritz Graf, Albert Henrichs, A. Hoekstra, Theo Korteweg, Gregory Nagy, Robert Parker, F. T. van Straten, and H. S. Versnel. Others who helped me in different ways are my brother Rolf, my mother-in-law Mrs. E. V. Bartlett, Peter Burian, Richard Kraut, Hans Teitler, and Sietze Wiersma. The support of the Netherlands Organization for the Advancement of Pure Research (Z.W.O.) enabled me to do part of my research at Oxford.

The final revisions and additions were written at the Center for Hellenic Studies in Washington D. C., and I owe grateful thanks to Bernard Knox for his help and advice, and for extending the hospitality of the center far beyond the time that was due to me.

ACKNOWLEDGMENTS

I should also like to thank Mrs. Joanna Hitchcock, Executive Editor of Princeton University Press, for her most pleasant co-operation and Rita Gentry for her meticulous and perspicacious editing.

Last but not least I thank Christine who kept me from always being busy with this study, and Benjamin and Melissa for their interest in "Daddy's book."

Abbreviations

THE BOOKS of the *Iliad* are referred to with Roman numerals, those of the *Odyssey* with Arabic ones. In addition the following abbreviations will be used.

Blass	F. W. Blass, *Lycurgi oratio in Leocratem* (Leipzig 1899).
Couvreur	P. Couvreur, *Hermiae Alexandrini in Platonis Phaedrum scholia* (Paris 1901).
Diels/Kranz	H. Diels and W. Kranz, *Die Fragmente der Vorsokratiker*, 6th ed., 3 vols. (Berlin 1951-52).
Edmonds	J. M. Edmonds, *The Fragments of Aristophanes*, vol. 1 (Leiden 1957).
Erbse	H. Erbse, *Untersuchungen zu den attizistischen Lexika* (Berlin 1950).
FGrH	F. Jacoby, *Die Fragmente der griechischen Historiker* (Berlin and Leiden 1923-).
Hense	O. Hense, *Teletis reliquiae*, 2nd ed. (Tübingen 1909).
Kahn	C. Kahn, *The Art and Thought of Heraclitus* (Cambridge 1979).
Kindstrand	J. F. Kindstrand, *Bion of Borysthenes* (Uppsala 1976).
Koerte	A. Koerte, *Menandri quae supersunt, pars altera*, 2nd ed. (Leipzig 1953).
Marcovich	M. Marcovich, *Heraclitus* (Merida 1967).

ABBREVIATIONS

Merkelbach/West	R. Merkelbach and M. L. West, *Fragmenta Hesiodea* (Oxford 1967).
Pfeiffer	R. Pfeiffer, *Callimachus*, vol. 1 (Oxford 1953).
Radt	S. Radt, *Tragicorum Graecorum fragmenta*, vol. 4 (Göttingen 1977).
RE	G. Wissowa et al., *Paulys Realencyclopädie der classischen Altertumswissenschaft* (Stuttgart and Munich 1894-).
RGVV	*Religionsgeschichtliche Versuche und Vorarbeiten* (Giessen, Berlin, and New York 1903-).
Rose	V. Rose, *Aristotelis qui ferebantur fragmenta librorum* (Leipzig 1886).
Snell/Maehler	B. Snell and H. Maehler, *Pindari carmina cum fragmentis*, 4th ed., vol. 2 (Leipzig 1975).
Voigt	E.-M. Voigt, *Sappho et Alcaeus* (Amsterdam 1971).
Wehrli	F. Wehrli, *Die Schule des Aristoteles*, 2nd ed., 10 vols. (Basel 1967-69), esp. vol. 2 *Aristoxenos* (1967); vol. 3 *Klearchos* (1969); vol. 7 *Herakleides Pontikos* (1969).
West	M. L. West, *Iambi et elegi Graeci*, vol. 1 (Oxford 1971).
ZPE	*Zeitschrift für Papyrologie und Epigraphik.*

The
Early Greek
Concept of
the Soul

One

THE SOUL

MODERN SECULARIZATION has made the salvation of the soul a problem of diminishing importance, but the prominence in Western society of psychiatry and psychology shows that we still care for our *psychē*, or "soul." Our idea of the soul has both eschatological and psychological attributes, and the borrowing of the Greek word *psychē* for modern terms implies that the Greeks viewed the soul in the modern way. Yet, when we look at Homer's epics we find that the word *psychē* has no psychological connotations whatsoever. And in Homer the *psychē* may fly away during a swoon or leave the body through a wound, behavior now not associated with the soul. Do these differences then suggest that the early Greeks viewed the soul and human psychological make-up differently?

Indeed, the Greeks of Homer did not yet have "cognisance of any concept denoting the psychic whole, of any notion that might correspond to our word 'soul,' " as Bruno Snell has demonstrated in his epoch-making book *The Discovery of the Mind*.[1] Moreover, the Greeks were not the only people who had a concept of the soul unlike our own. The Anglo-Saxon concept of *sawol*, the linguistic ancestor of the mod-

[1] B. Snell, *Die Entdeckung des Geistes*, 4th ed. (Göttingen 1975), English ed., *The Discovery of the Mind*, trans. T. G. Rosenmeyer (Oxford 1953). The summary of Snell's thesis is by H. Lloyd-Jones, *The Justice of Zeus* (Berkeley, London, and Los Angeles 1971) 9.

3

ern English word "soul," lacked any psychological content,[2] and the evidence we will consider below shows that this absence is common in the soul beliefs of most "primitive" peoples. Thus an analysis of the early Greek concept of the soul may not only contribute to a better understanding of the development of the Greek, and, consequently, the modern Western mind, but can also clarify the so-called primitive notion of the soul.

Such an analysis may look deceptively simple at first. After all, what needs to be done? We collect words normally translated as "soul" or those associated with it, and so are led, presumably, to the Greek concept. The Greek material has been approached repeatedly in this manner. However, scholars have failed to ask some important preliminary questions. First, should the term "soul" be used at all? It is now generally recognized that the use of modern Western terminology to describe non-Western beliefs influences analysis since it assumes the existence among other peoples of the same semantic fields for modern words, and thus often implies a nonexistent similarity.[3] In order to escape this danger a recent monograph introduced new terms to describe as exactly as possible the Oceanic concepts of the soul.[4] Although the use of modern Western terms can be

[2] See, e.g., *Beowulf* 801, 852, 2820 etc. For the cognate Old High German *seola*, see G. Becker, *Geist und Seele im Altsächsischen und im Althochdeutschen* (Heidelberg 1964).

[3] See H. Fischer, *Studien über Seelenvorstellungen in Ozeanien* (Munich 1965); J. G. Oosten, "The Examination of Religious Concepts in Religious Anthropology," in T. P. van Baaren and H.J.W. Drijvers (eds.), *Religion, Culture and Methodology* (The Hague and Paris 1973) 99-108. The problems arising from the use of such general terms as "soul" have been lucidly analyzed by the Dutch anthropologist Anton Blok, *Wittgenstein en Elias* (Amsterdam 1976).

[4] Fischer, *Studien über Seelenvorstellungen*. In his terminology Fischer was followed by L. Leertouwer, *Het beeld van de ziel bij drie Sumatraanse volken* (Diss. Univ. of Groningen 1977). Leertouwer's results, as do Fischer's, correspond with those reached by Arbman and his pupils.

misleading there are dangers inherent in the use of completely new terms. If every scholar introduces new terms to cover his specific area, from the Bongo-Bongo to ancient Greece, we will end up with a scientific Babel where communication is well-nigh impossible. For that reason I shall not introduce new terms for Greece but shall use the existing anthropological terminology. In so doing we shall, however, always have to be careful that we do not import into the Greek material shades of meaning that are typical of our own terms but not characteristic of the Greeks.

There is yet another problem to be faced. Scholars of the various soul beliefs have made extensive use of the insights of modern psychology in attempts to identify the experiences that moulded primeval man's ideas about himself. However, experiences are not events that take place in a historical vacuum. We recall and interpret our experience with the help of stereotypes of the particular society in which we live.[5] Our own experience therefore may well be vastly different from those of primeval man. Although it is difficult to reconstruct those primeval experiences, we can sometimes trace developments of concepts by studying the etymology of the words concerned—for example, of *psychē*. In that case, however, we must beware of introducing into our texts the etymologies we have discovered. The fact that *psychē* once had a connection with breath does not necessarily mean that it has this meaning in Homer. Our point of departure must always be the assumption that the meaning of a word can only be derived from its use in the language.

Classicists seem to be in a more favorable position than many students of social anthropology. Between them and their sources there is not an informant who has his own

[5] E. E. Evans-Pritchard, *Theories of Primitive Religion* (Oxford 1965) 24; K. Thomas, *Religion and the Decline of Magic*, 2nd ed. (Harmondsworth 1973) 104.

interests and opinions or who is too young to be fully acquainted with his people's tradition. Nor do classicists have to rely upon the data of only one or two reports, as do scholars of soul belief in North America and North Eurasia. Classical students can study their subject directly from the texts and monuments and thereby establish meaning from a word's context or through its comparison with similar representations or texts.

Yet classicists also have particular difficulties stemming from the nature of the sources. The archaeological remains and reports are not always as informative as we might wish. The ancient authors have their particular bias and do not give systematic accounts of their soul belief. We often have to glean our information from records where information on the soul appears only incidentally. Sometimes a concept or rite in the period under investigation can only be compared with one in a later document. Such later examples cannot bring absolute confirmation of an interpretation, although they can enhance its probability. In some cases we have to compare a subject with rites or concepts from other cultures. Again, such a comparison cannot constitute absolute proof, but it may establish a certain degree of probability, depending on the number and nature of the parallels.

Modern research on the early Greek idea of the soul started in 1894 when Nietzsche's friend Erwin Rohde published his *Psyche: The Cult of Souls and Belief in Immortality among the Greeks*, a supreme scholarly achievement, written with such skill that it soon became a classic.[6] Rohde

[6] E. Rohde, *Psyche: Seelencult und Unsterblichkeitsglaube der Griechen*, 2 vols., 1st ed. 1894, 2nd ed. (Freiburg, Leipzig, and Tübingen 1898), English ed., *Psyche: The Cult of Souls and Belief in Immortality Among the Greeks*, trans. W. B. Hillis (London 1925). For surveys of anthropological studies of soul belief, see Å. Hultkrantz, *Conceptions of the soul*

possessed a profound knowledge of the ancient Greek world and he developed his views in dialogue with contemporary anthropological and folkloric studies. He was much impressed with the ruling animistic theory that primitive man had conceived of the notion of the soul as a double of man when he observed that in dreams he could wander away.[7] Rohde tried to harmonize this view with the Homeric text but, as he could not find any instance of the soul as double in Homer, he resorted to a fragment of Pindar:

> In happy fate all die a death
> That frees from care,
> And yet there still will linger behind
> A living image of life,
> For this alone has come from the gods.
> It sleeps while the members are active;
> But to those who sleep themselves
> It reveals in myriad visions
> The fateful approach
> Of adversities or delights.[8]

This fragment indeed illustrates the theory that in dreams the soul acts as a double, but Rohde did not bother to explain why this activity does not occur in Homer; neither did he find it necessary to continue his analysis of the words used for "soul." Like the great majority of his contemporaries, he was exclusively interested in the destination of the soul, and had no eye for the rich and varied Homeric psychological terminology. His interpretation was enthusiastically received by some and silently rejected by others, particularly

---

among North American Indians (Stockholm 1953) 15-35; Fischer, *Studien über Seelenvorstellungen*, 1-44.

[7] H. Spencer, *The Principles of Sociology*, vol. 1 (London 1876) 147-157.

[8] Pindar fragment 131b Snell/Maehler, trans. W. Jaeger, *The Theology of the Early Greek Philosophers* (Oxford 1947) 75. I have added the (corrupt) fragment 131a, see F. Graf, *Eleusis und die orphische Dichtung Athens in vorhellenistischer Zeit*, *RGVV*, vol. 33 (Berlin and New York 1974) 86.

by the greatest classical scholar of that time, Wilamowitz,[9] but it remained the starting point for all subsequent discussions. These discussions did not make much fundamental progress toward an eschatology of the soul, but they rightly stressed the difference between the soul of the living and the dead, and took into account the etymology of the various words studied.[10] They did, moreover, advance our knowledge of the Homeric psychology of the soul, an advance culminating in Snell's demonstration that the early Greeks did not yet have a unitary concept of the body and mind.[11] Snell's analysis has been corrected, supplemented, and refined, but not superseded, by later scholars.[12] We still lack, however, a systematic approach that assembles all the

[9] For Wilamowitz's estimation of Rohde's *Psyche*, see now A. Henrichs, " 'Der Glaube der Hellenen': Religionsgeschichte als Glaubensbekenntnis und Kulturkritik," in W. M. Calder III and H. Flashar (eds.), *Wilamowitz nach 50 Jahren* (Darmstadt 1983).

[10] For the distinction, see W. F. Otto, *Die Manen oder von den Urformen des Totenglaubens* (Berlin 1923). G. Widengren, *Religionsphänomenologie* (Berlin 1969) 436 suggests that Otto was the first to make this distinction, but this had already been done by A. C. Kruyt, *Het animisme in den Indischen archipel* (The Hague 1906) 2. For the etymology, see E. Bickel, *Homerischer Seelenglaube* (Berlin 1925).

[11] Snell, *Gnomon* 7 (1931) 74-86 had first developed his views in a review of his most important predecessor in the field of Homeric psychology, J. Böhme, *Die Seele und das Ich im homerischen Epos* (Leipzig and Berlin 1929).

[12] See R. B. Onians, *The Origins of European Thought*, 2nd ed. (Cambridge 1954); A. Lesky, *Göttliche und menschliche Motivierung im homerischen Epos* (Heidelberg 1961); H. Fraenkel, *Dichtung und Philosophie des frühen Griechentums*, 2nd ed. (Munich 1962), English ed. *Early Greek Poetry and Philosophy*, trans. M. Hadas and J. Willis (Oxford 1975); M. P. Nilsson, *Geschichte der griechischen Religion*, 3rd ed., vol. 1 (Munich 1967) 193; A.W.H. Adkins, *From the Many to the One* (London 1970); W. J. Verdenius, "Archaische denkpatronen (pt.) 2," *Lampas* 3 (1970) 98-113, esp. 101-107 and "Archaische denkpatronen (pt.) 3," *Lampas* 5 (1972) 98-121, esp. 98-104; Lloyd-Jones, *The Justice of Zeus*, 8-10; K. J. Dover, *Greek Popular Morality in the Time of Plato and Aristotle* (Oxford 1974) 150-152.

elements and accounts for all the factors determining the
nouns for the different parts of what we usually associate
with the soul.

Such an integral approach was first undertaken by the
Swedish Sanskritist Ernst Arbman in an analysis of Vedic
soul belief in India. He found that the concept of the soul
(ātman, puruṣa) was preceded by a duality where the eschatological and psychological attributes of the soul had not
yet merged. For Christian Scandinavia and classical Greece
he arrived at the same conclusion. After these high cultures
he proceeded to investigate "primitive" ones, where he found
the same duality, although its presence had often been ob-
scured by the concept of the soul held by the field inves-
tigators themselves.[13]

In his analysis Arbman distinguished between body souls
endowing the body with life and consciousness and the free
soul, an unencumbered soul representing the individual
personality. The free soul is active during unconsciousness,
and passive during consciousness when the conscious individual replaces it. It is not exactly clear where the passive
free soul resides in the body. The body souls are active
during the waking life of the living individual. In contrast
to the free soul the body soul is often divided into several
parts. Usually it falls into two categories: one is the life soul,
frequently identified with the breath, the life principle; the
other is the ego soul. The body soul, or several of its parts,
represents the inner self of the individual. In the early stage
of the development of Vedic soul belief the free soul and
the body souls did not yet constitute a unity; later the concept of the Vedic free soul, ātman, incorporated the psy-

[13] E. Arbman, "Untersuchungen zur primitiven Seelenvorstellung mit
besonderer Rücksicht auf Indien," pts. 1-2, Le Monde Oriental 20 (1926)
85-222 and 21 (1927) 1-185.

chological attributes of the body souls, a development that occurred among a number of peoples.

Arbman's views have been elaborated by his pupils in two major monographs on the soul beliefs of North America and North Eurasia, confirmed by the studies of other scholars, and widely accepted by anthropologists.[14] It seems reasonable to apply his method to the problem of Greek soul belief in order to establish its value for the study of archaic Greek soul belief. This comparative analysis will begin with the epic tradition, the earliest and richest source, that greatly influenced later ideas, and will then consider material from the period after the epic until about 400 B.C. when aspects of Greek soul belief occur that are not found in Homer. In this way we can hope to see as complete a picture as possible of Greek soul belief before the soul became the subject of systematic reflection by Plato and other philosophers. Arbman concentrated especially on the soul of the living, but his pupils also paid attention (albeit to a much lesser degree) to the soul of the dead, of animals, and plants! These aspects of the Greek concept of the soul will be compared to the discoveries of Arbman's pupils to enrich our understanding of them.

This analysis necessarily has a certain ideal character. The evidence comes from different places, and we simply do not know whether all the aspects of the Greek soul belief

[14] See Hultkrantz, *Conceptions of the soul among North American Indians*; I. Paulson, *Die primitiven Seelenvorstellungen der nordeurasischen Völker* (Stockholm 1958); Å. Hultkrantz, "Seele," in K. Galling (ed.), *Die Religion in Geschichte und Gegenwart*, 3rd ed. (Tübingen 1961) 1634-1636; H. Hochegger, "Die Vorstellungen von 'Seele' und 'Totengeist' bei afrikanischen Völkern," *Anthropos* 60 (1965) 273-339; B. G. Alver, "Conceptions of the living human soul in the Norwegian tradition," *Temenos* 7 (1971) 7-33; J. Láng, "The Concept of Psyche," *Acta ethnographica academiae scientiarum Hungaricae* 22 (1973) 171-197; J. G. Oosten, *The Theoretical Structure of the Religion of the Netsilik and Iglulik* (Diss. Univ. of Groningen 1976) 30-41.

or of a rite can be found throughout the period under investigation and throughout Greece. There may well be local variants and developments that escape us because of the fragmentary nature of our sources. In addition since the records come mainly from the upper classes of Greek society, the ideas expressed there may not have been shared by the lower classes. The sources do not allow us to differentiate in this respect.

We discuss the material arranged as far as possible according to the categories defined by Arbman and his pupils, and then we compare the results with the concepts of Arbman described in detail at that point. In general the material will not be analyzed exhaustively but only so far as it is of interest for a better understanding of the Greek soul belief; the texts cited are offered by way of example. The analysis may seem somewhat dogmatic since in each case only a few examples are given as illustration, but for each term discussed an extensive bibliography is given to allow the reader to pursue the material at length.

This study then applies the model of "primitive" soul belief with its distinction between a free soul representing the individuality of a person and the body souls endowing a person with life and consciousness. Following this model *psychē* will be identified in the next chapter as corresponding with the free soul and terms connected with man's inner life such as *thymos, noos*, and *menos*, as corresponding with the body souls. Although the concept of *psychē* developed into the modern unitary soul, its "primitive" character can be discerned in the so-called shamanistic traditions and the early descriptions of dreams. An investigation of terminology in the last chapter will show that for the Greeks, as for many other peoples, the free soul of the living continued as the soul of the dead, although other manifestations of the deceased were also thought to exist. There was no uniform representation of the dead in an afterlife, neither did all the dead have the same status. An appendix will take up the question of the possible existence of a soul in plants and animals, and in a second appendix the wandering soul in Western European folktales will be discussed.

Finally, since the sources are fragmentary and hard to interpret; it may well be that others will be inclined to draw different conclusions from the material studied here. But I hope that in any case this archaeology of Greek anthropology will make a fresh start in the analysis of the early Greek concept of the soul.

Two

THE SOUL OF THE
LIVING

IN CHAPTER ONE we saw that Arbman distinguishes between a free soul representing the individual personality and the body souls endowing the body with life and consciousness. In this chapter we apply this distinction to the soul of the living in Homer and the Archaic Age. Homer distinguishes between a free soul, corresponding with *psychē*, and body souls, corresponding with *thymos, noos*, and *menos*. One element of Arbman's definition of the free soul, the activity of the soul in trance, we find only in the Archaic Age; yet it was an integral part of Greek dualistic soul belief and, contrary to Dodds' view (discussed below), was not derived from the shamanistic practices of the Siberians. Of Arbman's description of the body souls Homer knows only the ego soul but his representation of the inner self of the individual is much richer than Arbman's definition of the ego soul suggests. Moreover, besides the more abstract ego souls Homer presents organs, such as the lungs and the heart, that also have psychological attributes.

The presence of Arbman's distinction in Homer suggests that the dualistic soul belief existed also before the time of Homer. In both these periods the free soul, while representative of the individual, possessed no psychological at-

13

tributes. Though linked to the living, its major significance was still eschatological. In addition the etymology of *psyche*, the free soul in Homer, links it to Arbman's life soul and suggests that during the Homeric period the free soul was developing into Arbman's unitary soul. This development was still going on and had not yet reached the state in which *psyche* incorporated the psychological attributes of the ego soul. That development would reach its completion only at the end of the fifth century. After this general outline of the nature of the soul of the living we start our detailed discussion of the free soul and the body souls with *psyche*.[1]

The Free Soul

As noted above, the *psyche* in Homer can be identified with the free soul. It is only mentioned in Homer as part of the living person at times of crisis. The passages reveal that without *psyche* a person cannot survive. When the embassy of the Greek army beseeches Achilles to suppress his anger

---

[1] On *psyche*, see the literature quoted in Chapter One; O. Regenbogen, *Kleine Schriften* (Munich 1961) 1-26; E. L. Harrison, "Notes on Homeric Psychology," *Phoenix* 14 (1960) 63-80, esp. 75-77; J. Warden, "Ψυχή in Homeric Death Descriptions," *Phoenix* 25 (1971) 95-103; H. G. Ingenkamp, "Inneres Selbst und Lebensträger," *Rheinisches Museum* 118 (1975) 48-61; S. M. Darcus, "A Person's Relation to ψυχή in Homer, Hesiod, and the Greek Lyric Poets," *Glotta* 57 (1979) 30-39; B. C. Claus, *Toward the Soul* (New Haven and London 1981). The extended discussion of *psyche* by A. Schnaufer, *Frühgriechischer Totenglaube* (Hildesheim and New York 1970) has been shown to be rather unconvincing, see C. Sourvinou-Inwood, *Journal of Hellenic Studies* 92 (1972) 220-222. We may add that also Schnaufer's use of the concepts of survival and *lebender Leichnam* is highly uncritical. For these concepts, see M. T. Hodgen, *The Doctrine of Survivals* (London 1936); G. Widengren, "Evolutionistische Theorien auf dem Gebiet der vergleichenden Religionswissenschaft," in G. Lanczkowski (ed.), *Selbstverständnis und Wesen der Religionswissenschaft* (Darmstadt 1974) 87-113; G. Wiegelmann, "Der 'lebende Leichnam' im Volksbrauch," *Zeitschrift für Volkskunde* 62 (1966) 161-183.

and resume fighting, he complains that he is continually risking his *psychē* (IX.322). Agenor, summoning up his courage to face Achilles who is routing the Trojans, reflects that his opponent has only one *psychē* (XXI.569); when Achilles pursues Hector around Troy, the poet comments that the prize will be Hector's *psychē* (XXII.161).

The *psychē* leaves the body during swoons. These swoons are all described in a more or less similar way and have recently been analyzed in great detail;[2] one example may therefore suffice. When his friend Pelagon had pulled a spear from Sarpedon's thigh, "his *psychē* left him and a mist came down upon his eyes" (v.696).[3] Although it is not stated specifically, we assume that the *psychē* returned, since Sarpedon recovered immediately. In none of these instances of swooning, however, is the return of the *psychē* mentioned. This omission has been commented upon more than once and will be discussed below.[4]

When a person dies, the *psychē* leaves forever and departs to Hades. For example, when Hector had spoken his last words to Achilles, death overtook him and "his *psychē* fled from his limbs and went to Hades" (XXII.362). In these cases *psychē* is sometimes closely connected with the *aiōn*, the *force vitale*, or the source of vitality.[5] But unlike *psychē*, in

[2] Schnaufer, *Frühgriechischer Totenglaube*, 191-201; see also A. Nehring, "Homer's Description of Syncope," *Classical Philology* 42 (1947) 106-121.

[3] Swooning is called *lipopsycheō*, or "leaving of the soul," in the post-Homeric period as well, see Thucydides 4.12 etc.

[4] J. Böhme, *Die Seele und das Ich im homerischen Epos* (Leipzig and Berlin 1929) 100ff., and Schnaufer, *Frühgriechischer Totenglaube*, 200, suggest various solutions.

[5] E. Benveniste, "Expression indo-européenne de l'éternité," *Bulletin de la Société de Linguistique de Paris* 38 (1937) 103-112; G. Dumézil, "Jeunesse, éternité, aube," *Annales d'histoire économique et sociale* 10 (1938) 289-301 and "Le plus vieux nom arménien de 'jeune homme'," *Bulletin de la Société de Linguistique de Paris* 39 (1938) 185-193; E. Degani, Αἰών

Homer we do not find the *aiōn* connected with the elderly; it is only the young who possess it in its full power.[6] When Hera discusses the fate of Sarpedon with Zeus, she describes his death as the time "when *psychē* and *aiōn* have left him" (xvi.453). Odysseus, in his farewell speech to Polyphemus utters the wish that he could send him to Hades "robbed of his *psychē* and *aiōn*" (9.523f.). In Homer the *psychē* does not have any physical or psychological connections. It is not the "life-stuff" or "breath of life," descriptions which in any case are ill-defined by those who use them.[7] We can say only that when the *psychē* has left the body forever, it dies.

It has been argued that in Homer the *psychē* was located in the head, since the terms *psychē* and head are sometimes used interchangeably. Nestor describes pirates as people "risking their souls" (3.74), while Mentor describes the suitors of Penelope as "risking their heads" (2.237). In the prologue of the *Iliad* the poet speaks of Achilles' wrath sending many *psychai* to Hades (1.3).[8] The expression is used again later, but then the poet uses heads instead of souls (xi.55). The interchangeability of head and soul would also explain the custom of holding the head of the deceased during

da Omero ad Aristotele (Padua 1961) 29-43; Claus, *Toward the Soul*, 11-14. For the meaning "time," see A.-J. Festugière, *Etudes de philosophie grecque* (Paris 1971) 254-272. For the supposed meaning "(spinal) marrow," see A. A. Nikitas, *Würzburger Jahrbücher für die Altertumswissenschaft*, n.s. 4 (1978) 75-86.

[6] Contrary to expectation, Greek does not have a word for "young" that is etymologically connected with *aiōn* like other Indo-European languages such as the Sanskrit *yuvan*, Latin *iuvenis*, and English *young*, see M. Porzig, "Alt und Jung, Alt und Neu," in *Festschrift Albert Debrunner* (Bern 1954) 351-362.

[7] R. B. Onians, *The Origins of European Thought*, 2nd ed. (Cambridge 1954) 109-116 on "life-stuff"; W. J. Verdenius, "Archaische denkpatronen (pt.) 2," *Lampas* 3 (1970) 105 on the "breath of life."

[8] An ancient variant reads "heads" instead of "souls!" See R. Pfeiffer, *History of Classical Scholarship* (Oxford 1968) 147f.

mourning (xxiv.712, 724), the primal offering (iii.273), and the importance of sneezing.[9] Yet it is obvious that the fact the head and *psychē* are sometimes used interchangeably does not necessarily lead to the conclusion that the *psychē* was located in the head. It can also mean that they represent the same thing, that is, the whole person. The only valid conclusion to be drawn from the association is that the Greeks considered the head as very important, which, in itself, is not very surprising. What we know for certain about the *psychē*'s location is merely that it flew away from the limbs (xvi.856; xxii.362),[10] or left the body through the mouth (ix.409), the chest (xvi.505), or through a wound in the flank (xiv.518).[11] That is all Homer says of a positive nature about the *psychē*.

How does this all compare with the free soul? As outlined by Arbman and his pupils the free soul is the individual's nonphysical mode of existence not only after death but also in dreams, swoons, and other types of unconsciousness. It

[9] Onians, *The Origins of European Thought*, 95-104. His view has been accepted by J. Warden, "Ἴφθιμος: A Semantic Analysis," *Phoenix* 23 (1969) 153-157 and Verdenius, "Archaische denkpatronen (pt.) 2," 105; but see also Claus, *Toward the Soul*, 61f.

[10] The Greek word *rhētea* is sometimes, probably wrongly, translated as "mouth," see Regenbogen, *Kleine Schriften*, 14; Verdenius, "Archaische denkpatronen (pt.) 2," 113.

[11] A number of peoples have thought the free soul resided in the eye in the form of a homunculus. This idea could have existed in early Greece, but we have only two testimonies for *psychē* departing from the eye and they both date from the later Roman empire. However, the double meaning of *korē* as "girl" and "pupil of the eye" may be a survival of this belief, see Babrius 95.35; W. Peek, *Griechische Versinschriften*, vol. 1 (Berlin 1955) no. 1166; Rohde, *Psyche* 1: 23 n. 1; K. F. Smith, "Pupula duplex," in *Studies in Honour of B. L. Gildersleeve* (Baltimore 1902) 287-300; E. Monseur, "L'âme pupilline," *Revue de l'histoire des religions* 51 (1905) 1-23; H. Bächtold-Stäubli (ed.), *Handwörterbuch des deutschen Aberglaubens*, vol. 1 (1927) 695-697; W. Déonna, "L'âme pupilline et quelques monuments," *L'Antiquité classique* 26 (1957) 59-90 and *Le Symbolisme de l'oeil* (Paris 1965) 30-35.

is the free soul in these conditions that represents a person's individuality. This is shown by the many tales in which people relate, as their personal experience, the adventures of their dream soul, whether in the shape of an insect, animal, or homunculus (Appendix Two). The free soul, therefore, is always active outside the body; it is not bound to it like the body souls. But precisely because the free soul functions outside the body its place inside the body is rather obscure, for when its owner is awake the body represents the individual and only its activities are of interest. The free soul in this state is only passively present and is not usually mentioned. Its exact place in the body is, for that reason, a matter of minor importance, though the location is often a source of speculation. In North Eurasia, for example, the free soul can be located throughout the body, or in the heart, the lungs, or the kidneys.[12] The free soul never has any physical or psychological attributes; it only represents the individual. In addition it is impossible for the free soul to continue its worldly existence when the body is dead even though it is always active outside the body. The soul cannot stay behind in a dead body but has to pursue an afterlife. In the same way the body is dependent upon the free soul. When the free soul disappears, the body dies after falling ill or gradually pines away.[13]

When we compare this description of the free soul with the Homeric *psychē*, one feature is conspicuously absent. In Homer the *psychē* does not represent a person's individuality in dreams or in forms of unconsciousness. Yet from

[12] I. Paulson, *Die primitiven Seelenvorstellungen der nordeurasischen Völker* (Stockholm 1958) 273-276.

[13] E. Arbman, "Untersuchungen zur primitiven Seelenvorstellung mit besonderer Rücksicht auf Indien," pt. 1, *Le Monde Oriental* 20 (1926) 97-117; Å. Hultkrantz, *Conceptions of the soul among North American Indians* (Stockholm 1953) 241-291; Paulson, *Die primitiven Seelenvorstellungen*, 266-303.

this absence we should not conclude that such a role for the *psychē* did not exist in Homer's time. Such a conclusion, drawn by Walter F. Otto, Rohde's fiercest critic, completely misconstrues the evidence. In Homer we find only a very special kind of dream and dream description. The dreams in Homer are "literary dreams" used to further the story and, as such, cannot be taken as informing about the whole real dream-experience of the early Greeks.[14] Homer's dream-descriptions always follow a strict pattern that may be divided into four stages:

1. Circumstance before the dream;
2. The dream image moving toward the sleeper and standing above the sleeper's head;[15]
3. The speech of the dream image;
4. The aftermath of the dream.[16]

This strict patterning was also the rule in the ancient Near East although there we find different introductory and concluding stages also followed by Herodotus.[17] Dreams in Ho-

[14] A. Kessels, *Studies on the Dream in Greek Literature*, 2nd ed. (Utrecht 1978) 2.

[15] The most frequently used term is *ephistēmi*, "to stand over," for which the material runs from Homer to the Byzantine Age, see L. Deubner, *De incubatione* (Leipzig 1900) 11, 71, 83, 89; A. Wikenhauser, "Die Traum-gesichte des Neuen Testaments in religionsgeschichtlicher Sicht," in T. Klauser and A. Ruecher (eds.), *Pisciculi, Festschrift Franz Joseph Döl-ger* (Münster 1939) 320-333; E. R. Dodds, *The Greeks and the Irrational* (Berkeley and Los Angeles 1951) 105, 123 n. 18; L. Robert, *Hellenica* 11-12 (1960) 544; F. T. van Straten, "Daikrates' Dream. A votive relief from Kos, and some other kat' onar dedications," *Bulletin Antieke Beschaving* 51 (1976) 1-38, esp. 30-32.

[16] Kessels, *Studies on the Dream*, 134f. whose analysis I have slightly simplified.

[17] A. L. Oppenheim, *The Interpretation of Dreams in the Ancient Near East, Transactions of the American Philosophical Society*, vol. 46, pt. 3 (Philadelphia 1956) 187: the dream consists "of an introduction which tells about the dreamer, the locality and other circumstances of the dream which were considered of import. The actual report of the dream-content

mer are neither fantastic nor incoherent because, presumably, this would make them very hard to use for literary purposes. Homer only reports those dreams with a message. The "message" dream as a "theological" event and as a literary topos "goes back to an age-old dream pattern, that of the incubation dream. Actual incubation dreams are quite rare in the texts of the ancient Near East, but the 'message' dream is most easily explained as a literary creation based upon transformed actual dream experiences of persons passing the night, after due ritual preparation, in the cella of the god's sanctuary in order to receive his command or advice. Only divine messages obtained under such circumstances are considered theologically—or politically, whichever the context demands—valid and genuine."[18] It is obvious that the "message" dream must have been especially popular with state leaders as a means of sanctioning political decisions since it would not require the help of an interpreter to understand them, which might be the case with dreams of travelling and seeing strange people.[19] Thus we conclude that, although we do not find in Homer the activities of a dream soul, its absence does not necessarily presuppose its nonexistence. We simply do not know.[20] It should

follows and is succeeded by the final part of the 'frame' which describes the end of the dream and often includes a section referring to the reaction of the dreaming person or, also, to the actual fulfilment of the prediction or promise contained in the dream." Patterning also occurs in *Genesis* 40, see W. Richter, "Traum und Traumdeutung im AT," *Biblische Zeitschrift* 7 (1963) 202-220. For Herodotus, see P. Frisch, *Die Träume bei Herodot* (Meisenheim 1968) 66-71. For anthropological examples of patterning, see B. Kilborne, "Pattern, Structure, and Style in Anthropological Studies of Dreams," *Ethos* 9 (1981) 165-185.

[18] A. L. Oppenheim, "Mantic Dreams in the Ancient Near East," in G. E. von Grunebaum and R. Caillois (eds.), *The Dream and Human Societies* (Berkeley and Los Angeles 1966) 341-350, esp. 348.

[19] Oppenheim, "The Interpretation of Dreams," 226f.

[20] J. Hundt, *Der Traumglaube bei Homer* (Greifswald 1935) 30 reached a similar conclusion. We may compare the observation of Robert Lowie,

also be noted that modern legends relating the adventures of the soul are not to be found in fine literature, like the *Iliad*, but mainly in folktales (Appendix Two).

A comparison of Arbman's description of the free soul with what we know about the Homeric *psychē* reveals the following similarities:

1. Both are located in an unspecified part of the body;
2. Both are inactive (and unmentioned) when the body is active;
3. Both leave the body during a swoon;
4. Both have no physical or psychological connections;
5. Both are a precondition for the continuation of life;
6. Both represent the individual after death.

Taken separately these similarities do not prove anything. As a whole, however, they provide for the existence of a free soul in Homeric Greece. Moreover, given the fact that the concept of the free soul seems to have existed at one time nearly everywhere for which we have evidence it is not unreasonable to infer that the Homeric *psychē* corresponds with the free soul.

Not only can *psychē* in Homer be identified with the customary functions of Arbman's free soul, but an examination of its etymology reveals that it expresses a stage in the development of the unitary soul. It is generally agreed that *psychē* is etymologically connected with *psychēin*, "to blow or to breathe."[21] This meaning is suggested in Homer when

---

Anthropological Papers. American Museum of Natural History 25 (1922) 342; he never succeeded in securing a detailed narrative of an ordinary dream among the North American Indians because his informants would report only visions.

[21] See H. Frisk, *Griechisches etymologisches Wörterbuch*, 2 vols. (Heidelberg 1960-1970) s.v. *psychē*; P. Chantraine, *Dictionnaire étymologique de la langue grecque*, 4 vols. (Paris 1968-1980) s.v. *psychē*. To Plato *Cratylus* 399 D, E and other ancient evidence for the connection, now add

the *psychē* leaves the body at the beginning of a swoon and then breathing begins again at the end.[22] Especially interesting in this connection is the description of Andromache's swoon where it is said that she "breathed forth" (*ekapusse*) her *psychē* (XXII.467), a word most likely connected with smoke.[23] Yet the absence of *psychē* at the end of the swoon recalls the concept of the free soul as defined by Arbman and his pupils. The movement of the person who had fainted proves that the soul has returned, and when the person is awake the free soul is of no further interest.

The Homeric poems are the culmination of a tradition of oral composition joining elements of different periods.[24] Their coexistence implies that we must be prepared to find different stages in the evolution of words and concepts without always being able to distinguish with certainty between older and younger elements. The etymology of *psychē* and the fact that the meaning "breath" is most prominent in the rather formulaic swoon descriptions imply that those cases in Homer where *psychē* has lost or is losing its purely physical meaning are later developments.

The original meaning of "breath" may well be an important clue to the better understanding of *psychē*'s development. As pointed out in Chapter One, Arbman also identified a life soul, usually associated with the breath, in which case he calls it a breath soul. According to Arbman the life soul

the recently excavated gold leaf from Hipponion, line 4; for a text of this gold leaf, see, e.g., S. Cole, "New Evidence for the Mysteries of Dionysos," *Greek, Roman, and Byzantine Studies* 21 (1980) 223-238, esp. 225.

[22] Verdenius, "Archaische denkpatronen 2," 105, 112 n. 67; also see Claus, *Toward the Soul*, 96f.

[23] Chantraine, *Dictionnaire étymologique*, s.v. *kapnos*.

[24] This is the convincing thesis of A. M. Snodgrass, "An Historical Homeric Society?" *Journal of Hellenic Studies* 94 (1974) 114-125, whose individual arguments, however, are open to objections, see M. I. Finley, *Economy and Society in Ancient Greece*, ed. B. D. Shaw and R. P. Saller (London 1981) 296; W. Donlan, *Classical World* 75 (1982) 146 n. 18.

often acquires new qualities and frequently develops into a unitary, that is, a modern type of soul. The Swedish anthropologist Hultkrantz, one of Arbman's most gifted pupils, has analyzed this process from a psychological viewpoint:

The breath-soul is the soul of great possibilities. It is at one and the same time material and immaterial, bound by matter and yet free. When Wundt combined the breath-soul with the idea of the free-soul, he did so on good grounds: both are unsubstantial and unstable. From the psychological viewpoint the conception of the free-soul is of course identical with the memory-image of the dead person projected to the supernatural reality; and the airy, etherial shape of the deceased is like a condensation of human breath. The surviving soul and the breath-soul thus have qualifications favouring a meeting and merging. But the fusion takes place only when the situation is suitable for this—when speculation has started or the dualistic front has been weakened. . . . it appears probable that the life-soul, in its character a breath-soul, has emancipated itself from its immediate physical functions and in consequence of its airy consistency been assimilated with and finally absorbed the conception of the free-soul.[25]

Such a process in which the original free soul becomes absorbed by the breath soul that, in turn, develops into a unitary soul, can be traced in the development of the Athapascan *nezacl*, Indian *ātman*, Estonian *hing*, Finnish *henki*, Russian *dusa*, and Wogulian *lili*.[26] A similar development is also likely for Latin *anima*, "breath," or free soul. However, it would be highly unusual to find that the breath

[25] Hultkrantz, *Conceptions of the soul*, 205, 206.

[26] Arbman, "Untersuchungen zur primitiven Seelenvorstellung," pt. 1, 203-211; Hultkrantz, *Conceptions of the soul*, 204-208; Paulson, *Die primitiven Seelenvorstellungen*, 245-252. Hultkrantz, *Conceptions of the soul*, 93 on *nezacl*; Arbman, "Untersuchungen zur primitiven Seelenvorstellung," pt. 2, 175ff. on *ātman*, with the critique of H. W. Bodewitz, *Vedische voorstellingen omtrent de 'ziel'* (Leiden 1978); O. Loorits, *Grundzüge des estnischen Volksglaubens*, vol. 1 (Stockholm 1949) 182f. on *hing*; Paulson, *Die primitiven Seelenvorstellungen*, 40 on *henki*, 248 on *lili*, and 367f. on *dusa*.

represents personal identity for, as a Hungarian anthropologist observed: "Not a single example did we find in the beliefs of more than 200 peoples to indicate that the breath left the body during sleep and that its adventures appeared as dreams, nor is it believed anywhere that the breath resembles human beings."[27] It is hard to see why the Greeks should form an exception.

All factors suggest, with due qualification, that the development from the life soul to the unitary soul, as sketched by Hultkrantz, also took place in early Greece. Before Homer the Greeks in all probability had a word for the free soul that was gradually replaced by the life soul, identified with the *psychē* or "breath," and that at the same time started to lose its purely physical function.[28] In Homer we meet this process at a halfway stage. *Psychē* has already absorbed the role of the free soul as the soul of the dead, but it has not lost all of its connections with its original function as breath. It was to be some centuries before *psychē* developed completely into a unitary soul.[29]

Can we find the free soul in post-Homeric times too? Archaic Age legends of persons whose souls were reputed to wander away during a trance indeed reflect the continuation of the belief in the free soul found in Homer. E. R. Dodds, on the contrary, thought that these legends revealed

[27] J. Láng, "The Concept of Psyche," *Acta ethnographica academiae scientiarum Hungaricae* 22 (1973) 189; for similar conclusions, see Hultkrantz, *Conceptions of the soul*, 479 and Fischer, *Studien über Seelenvorstellungen*, 315-320. This has been insufficiently taken into account by W. Burkert, *Griechische Religion der archaischen und klassischen Epoche* (Stuttgart 1977) 301-303.

[28] Láng, "The Concept of Psyche," 189f. infers the same development without noticing its parallels.

[29] See V. N. Jarkho, "Zum Menschenbild der nachhomerischen Dichtung," *Philologus* 112 (1968) 147-172, esp. 148-151; Verdenius, "Archaische denkpatronen 3," 98-100; Darcus, "A Person's Relation to ψυχή"; Claus, *Toward the Soul*, 69-102.

a new and revolutionary conception of the relation between body and soul appearing at the end of the Archaic Age. According to him, this new development was due to trade and colonization that had brought the Greeks in contact with the shamanistic culture of the Black Sea Scythians in the seventh century; he had been inspired by a celebrated article on Scythian shamanism by the Swiss Karl Meuli, who, for a classical scholar, possessed an unusual knowledge of North Eurasian beliefs and customs.[30] Dodds' and Meuli's views have been highly influential and not only the wandering soul but also other elements of these legends have been derived from Central or North Asia. In our analysis we shall inquire whether the wandering of the soul indeed has to be ascribed to a shamanistic influence or whether these legends are testimonies of authentic Greek soul belief.

Evidence of a soul wandering away in a trance is found in legends about two men, Aristeas of Proconnesus, an island in the Propontis later called Marmara, and Hermotimos of Clazomenae, a town on the west coast of Asia Minor. Herodotus (4.14) tells the following local legend of Aristeas:

They say that Aristeas, a member of one of the noblest families of the city, entered a fuller's shop in Proconnesus and dropped dead. The fuller closed his shop and left to inform the relatives of the dead man. When the story had already spread about the town that Aristeas was dead, an inhabitant of Cyzicus, who came from Artace, arrived and started to dispute with those who said this, asserting that he had met Aristeas, who was on his way to Cyzicus, and had spoken with him. So this man strenuously contradicted the rumor; but the relatives had arrived at the shop with the things

---

[30] Dodds, *The Greeks and the Irrational*, 135-178; K. Meuli, "Scythica," *Hermes* 70 (1935) 121-176, reprinted in Meuli, *Gesammelte Schriften*, 2 vols. (Basel and Stuttgart 1975) 2: 817-879. For Dodds, see his autobiography *Missing Persons* (Oxford 1977); G. Mangani, "Sul metodo di Eric Dodds e sulla nozione di 'irrazionale,'" *Quaderni di Storia* no. 11 (1980) 173-205. For Meuli, see the bibliography by Bremmer, in G. Piccaluga (ed.), *Perennitas. Studi in onore di Angelo Brelich* (Rome 1980) 68 n. 5.

due for the funeral, intending to carry away the body. When the shop was opened, however, Aristeas did not appear to be there, neither dead nor alive. After six years he appeared in Proconnesus and composed that poem which the Greeks call *Arimaspea*, after which composition he disappeared for the second time. This is what those cities relate.

In his poem Aristeas told how he, possessed by Apollo, travelled to the far north to the country of the Issedones and learned from them about the Hyperboreans living near the sea (Herodotus 4.14) and the one-eyed Arimaspi who stole gold from griffins (Herodotus 3.116). That was, however, not yet the end of Aristeas for Herodotus (4.15) goes on:

What follows I know to have happened to the people of Metapontum in Italy two hundred and forty years after the second disappearance of Aristeas, as I found by calculations made in Metapontum and Proconnesus. The Metapontines say that Aristeas appeared in person in their country and ordered them to erect an altar to Apollo and near to it a statue bearing the name of Aristeas the Proconnesian. Apollo, he told them, had come to them alone of the Italiotes; and he accompanied the god at the time, being now in the shape of Aristeas, but then, when he accompanied the god, in the shape of a raven. After these words he vanished, but the Metapontines say that they sent to Delphi to ask the god what the apparition signified. The Pythia ordered them to obey the apparition: it would be better for them if they obeyed. They accepted this and did as they were told, so there is now a statue bearing the name of Aristeas, close by the image of Apollo, and laurel bushes are standing around it.

The raven is also mentioned by Pliny (*Natural History* 7.174) who in telling how the soul of Aristeas was seen flying from his mouth in the shape of a raven seems to combine the Metapontine and the earlier legend.

Apollonius gives us a second description of a soul wandering away during a trance in the tale of Hermotimos (*Mirabilia* 3):

They say that the soul of Hermotimos of Clazomenae, wandering apart from the body, was absent for many years, and in different places foretold events such as great floods and droughts and also earthquakes and plagues and the like, while his stiff body was lying inert, and that the soul, after certain periods re-entering the body as into a sheath, aroused it. As he did this often, and although his wife had orders from him that, whenever he was going to be in trance (lit. to depart) nobody should touch his 'corpse,' neither one of the citizens nor anybody else, some people went into his house and, having moved his weak wife by entreaty, they gazed at Hermotimos lying on the ground, naked and motionless. They took fire and burned him, thinking that the soul, when it should arrive and have no place anymore to enter, would be completely deprived of being alive—which indeed happened. The inhabitants of Clazomenae honor Hermotimos till the present day and a sanctuary for him has been founded into which no woman enters for the reason above given.

Many details of this account have disappeared in Pliny's *Natural History* (7.174), so that we can discern the reductionist tendency discussed below, even though it contains the "superfluous" detail of the enemies' name: "We find that the soul of Hermotimos of Clazomenae used to leave his body and roam abroad, and in its wanderings report to him from a distance many things that only one present at them could know of—his body in the meantime being half-conscious, until finally some enemies named the Cantharidae burned his body and so deprived his soul upon its return of what may be called its sheath."

Pliny's version of Hermotimos' wandering soul is already much less informative than Apollonius' report. Differences like these induced C. W. von Sydow, a Swedish folklorist with a great interest in the formal aspects of popular traditions, to introduce the terms "memorate" and "fabulate," terms that have been generally accepted by German and Scandinavian scholars but neglected by the Anglo-Saxon world.[31] Von Sydow defined a memorate as the story of people about their own, strictly personal, experiences. This definition, although in principle very useful, has proved to be somewhat too narrow.[32] The memorate can best be defined as the report of a supranormal experience either of the narrator himself or of one of his acquaintances. Legends that do not relate strictly personal experiences Von Sydow called "fabulates"; these need not have a basis in the folk belief of the region from which the tale comes. Memorates can relate highly individual experiences in which traditional concepts play only a minor role, but they are more often dominated by such concepts that then give the stories a stereotyped character: the ghosts people meet are always dressed in white![33] Over time and distance memorates can become transformed and standardized. Details unnecessary for the story but typical of the narrator are dropped and other motifs are added. The exact time and place, the situation and frequency of an experience, the interpretation of the narrator himself, or the reaction of his audience are often ignored. The social context of the happening remains vague. In this way the memorates become migratory legends of only minor importance as testimonies for the beliefs of a certain region.[34]

[31] C. W. von Sydow, *Selected Papers on Folklore* (Copenhagen 1948) 73-77, reprinted in L. Petzoldt (ed.), *Vergleichende Sagenforschung* (Darmstadt 1969) 78-81; see also L. Dégh and A. Vászonyi, "The Memorate and the Proto-Memorate," *Journal of American Folklore* 87 (1974) 225-239. For Von Sydow, see G. Berg, "Cor Wilhelm von Sydow (1878-1952)," *Arv* 25-26 (1969-1970) 171-188.

[32] See L. Honko, "Memorates and the Study of Folk Beliefs," *Journal of the Folklore Institute* 1 (1964) 5-19, reprinted in Petzoldt (ed.), *Vergleichende Sagenforschung*, 287-306.

[33] J. Pentikäinen, "Grenzprobleme zwischen Memorat und Sage," *Temenos* 3 (1968) 136-167.

[34] G. Granberg, "Memorat und Sage, einige methodische Gesichtspunkte," in Petzoldt (ed.), *Vergleichende Sagenforschung*, 90-98.

The legends of Aristeas and Hermotimos are still remarkably detailed and they can therefore be accepted as memorates from the Archaic Age; the reports are testimonies of the soul belief of that period whether they are considered to be originally Greek or derived from a shamanistic culture. Aristeas' legend reveals one aspect of the free soul not found in Homer, the wandering of the soul in a trance. This becomes clear when we subject his legend to a detailed analysis; we start with the trance.[35]

It seems reasonable to assume that Aristeas' supposed death was a deep trance, since he disappeared afterwards and returned after many years. This identification of death and trance occurs in very different cultures; an interesting example is given by the English traveller Richard Johnson in a description of a Samoyed shamanistic séance in 1556. After the shaman had started to play the drum and put on his garment, "hee singeth as wee use heere in Englande to hallow, whope, or showte at houndes, and the rest of the company answere him with this Owtis, Igha, Igha, Igha, and the Priest replieth againe with his voyces. And they answere him with the selfsame wordes so manie times that in the ende he becommeth as it were madde, and falling downe as hee were dead, having nothing on him but a shirt, lying upon his backe I might perceive him to breathe."[36] In an account of the activities of a Lapp shaman, it is observed

[35] For Aristeas, see J.D.P. Bolton, *Aristeas of Proconnesus* (Oxford 1962); Burkert, *Gnomon* 35 (1963) 235-240, and *Lore and Science in Ancient Pythagoreanism* (Cambridge, Mass. 1972) 147-149; Meuli, *Gesammelte Schriften* 2: 853-864. For Proconnesus, see L. Robert, *Monnaies grecques* (Geneva 1967) 15-22.

[36] R. Hakluyt, *The Principal Navigations, Voyages, Traffiques and Discoveries of the English Nation*, 1st ed. 1589 (London 1927) 354. Johnson shows himself here to be a more perceptive observer than Bogoras (note 56) who saw in this singing only hysteria, see Meuli, *Gesammelte Schriften*, 2: 823 n. 1.

that he "worked for a while with the gabdes (Lapp drum) and with one finger followed the signs to be found on it. Suddenly he stretched himself out on his back and lay as if dead for a quarter of an hour. They could not even see that he was breathing."[37] Among North American Indians we find the same practice. The ecstatic is said to be "like dead" or even "to be dead."[38] The identification also takes place in a nonshamanistic context. When the Irish abbot Furseus (ca. 650) once awoke from an ecstasy, he saw around him his relatives and neighbors, all assembled to lament his death.[39] And the Italian monk Filippo Neri (1515-1595) was awakened by the extreme unction that his colleague, Father Bordini, administered to him.[40] During the great Ghost Dance movement in America at the turn of this century a woman lapsed into a deep trance lasting for such a long time that people thought she was dead.[41] She awoke only when she had been laid to rest on a platform according to the traditional rites.[42]

Aristeas did not reach his ecstasy by a definite technique,

[37] E. Arbman, *Ecstasy or Religious Trance*, vol. 2 (Uppsala 1963) 108.

[38] Hultkrantz, *Conceptions of the soul*, 280.

[39] *Acta Sanctorum, Januarii tomus secundus*, ed. J. Bollandus (Antwerp 1643) day 16, 403 chap. 32.

[40] F. Pösl, *Das Leben des heiligen Philippus Neri, Stifter der Congregation des Oratoriums in Italien*, 2nd ed. (Regensburg 1857) 271.

[41] Arbman, *Ecstasy*, 103f. The classic study of the Ghost Dance movement is J. Mooney, *The Ghost Dance and the Sioux Outbreak of 1890* (Washington, D.C., 1896); for modern views, see B. Wilson, *Magic and the Millennium*, 2nd ed. (London 1975) 292-308; T. W. Overholt, "Short Bull, Black Elk, Sword, and the 'meaning' of the Ghost Dance," *Religion* 8 (1978) 171-195. For a photo of such a trance, see Mooney, pl. 118; also in Å. Hultkrantz, *Prairie and Plains Indians*, Iconography of Religion vol. 10, pt. 2 (Leiden 1973) pl. 45b.

[42] For illustrations of this kind of Indian burial, see Hultkrantz, *Prairie and Plains Indians*, pl. 40-43; Meuli, *Gesammelte Schriften* 2, pl. 75f.; H. Lang, *Indianer waren meine Freunde. Leben und Werk Karl Bodmers* (Bern and Stuttgart 1976) 41.

like Hermotimos (below); instead he evidently was unable to control himself, since he very suddenly fell into a trance in the fuller's shop. This lack of control is not uncommon among ecstatics and also occurred among Christian saints. Filippo Neri fell into trance when he gave absolution, and Caterina Ricci (1522-1554) had to be given special rules by her monastery because her sudden ecstasies created too much disruption of normal life.[43]

Having looked at the trance of Aristeas, we shall now discuss the wandering of his soul that caused his miraculous appearance on the road to Cyzicus. The appearance belongs to a familiar type of folktale in which a person who is fast asleep, lies in trance or is dying, is at the same time seen in a different place.[44] For example, a Tirolean folktale recounts how "at Mieders in Stubai a farmer once was at the point of dying. A day-labourer saw the same man raking leaves outside the village and thought: look at that, the fellow is healthy again! Just when the day-labourer came into the village, the death-bell tolled and he asked who had died. How surprised he was at the news that it was the farmer he had just seen outside raking leaves."[45]

The theme is applied more subtly in a Swedish folktale set in the mid-eighteenth century:

When a Swedish court could not start because the magistrate had not arrived, a naite (a Lappshaman) was asked to find out what delayed him. He went into trance and, when woken up, told "that the magistrate had taken the wrong way and got stuck in a drift. But now he was on the right road again and would arrive in three

[43] Pösl, *Leben des heiligen Philippus Neri*, 271; H. Bayonne, *Vie de sainte Catherine de Ricci de Florence*, vol. 1 (Paris 1873) 308.

[44] W. Peuckert, *Verborgenes Niedersachsen* (Göttingen 1960) 11-35; V. Meyer-Matheis, *Die Vorstellung eines alter ego in Volkserzählungen* (Diss. Univ. of Freiburg 1973) 5-64.

[45] J. A. Heyl, *Volkssagen, Bräuche und Meinungen aus Tirol* (Brixen, Austria 1897) 72.

hours." And sure enough, in three hours he did arrive; and he then related that he had taken quite the wrong road and the sledge had finally tipped over and got stuck, so that he had had a great deal of trouble getting it loose again. "And we should have been there still if an old Same (Lapp) had not chanced to come and help us. He was, by the way, an uncommonly strong fellow, that Same" said the magistrate. But just then he caught sight of the naite and said "Are you here now? But it was you who helped us?" "It was" said the naite.[46]

An example of bilocation during sleep appears in St. Augustine who records the following event without giving it a date nor ascribing it to any known philosopher:

Another man also said that in his own home, at night before he went to bed, he saw a certain philosopher whom he knew very well, coming to him, and this philosopher expounded to him some Platonic theories that he had refused to explain when he was earlier asked to do so. And when the same philosopher was asked afterwards why he did in another's house what he had refused to do for him when the request was made in his own house, he said: "I did not do it, but I dreamed that I did."[47]

So whereas the philosopher thought that he expounded the Platonic theories only in his dream, the other man saw him in person.

The occasions of bilocation—sleep, trance, and death— are those when the free soul leaves the body, and it seems very likely that the key to this type of story is to be found in the concept of the free soul. Because the free soul, that is, in primitive experience the whole person, was believed to leave the body and to experience adventures, it is understandable that, at the same time, it was believed to be visible during these journeys outside the body. The story

[46] Arbman, *Ecstasy*, 106; for soul journeys of Lapp shamans, also see R. T. Christiansen, "Noai'der og Finnferd," *Sameliv* (1951-52) 51-61.

[47] Augustine, *De Civitate Dei* 18.18, trans. E. M. Sandford and W. M. Green, *Saint Augustine, The City of God against the Pagans* (London and Cambridge, Mass. 1965) 427.

about Aristeas points therefore in the direction of the existence of the concept of the free soul in Archaic Greece.

Bilocation reportedly took place in antiquity and also in more modern times but in a number of cases the exact circumstances remain obscure. Of Pythagoras it was told only that he was seen in Croton and Metapontum at the same hour on the same day, a feat later imitated by Apollonius of Tyana who was seen in Smyrna and Ephesos on the same day.[48] St. Francis was seen in Arles blessing the brethren when he was sitting at the same time on the mountain La Verna; Filippo Neri himself told how he was present at the death of his friend Cordella even though he did not leave his own room.[49]

Rohde saw in the death and disappearance of Aristeas a

[48] Aelian *Varia Historia* 2.26, 4.17; Apollonius *Mirabilia* 6; Iamblichus *Life of Pythagoras* 134, 136 (Metapontum and Tauromenium); Philostratus *Life of Apollonius* 4.10 (Thurii and Metapontum; the feat of Apollonius). For Apollonius and Pythagoras, see E. L. Bowie, "Apollonius of Tyana: Tradition and Reality," in W. Haase (ed.), *Aufstieg und Niedergang der römischen Welt*, ser. 2, vol. 16, pt. 2 (Berlin and New York 1978) 1652-1699.

[49] Thomas de Celano, *Vita prima S. Francisci Assisiensis*, 1st ed., 1228 (Quaracchi 1926) 53; H. Thode, *Franz von Assisi und die Anfänge der Kunst der Renaissance in Italien*, 4th ed. (Vienna 1934) pl. 24f.; Pösl, *Leben des heiligen Philippus Neri*, 263. Compare also E. Benz, *Die Vision* (Stuttgart 1969) 210: "Zu den auffälligsten para-psychischen Phänomenen, die sich im Erfahrungsbereich der Visionäre zeigten, gehört das Phänomen der Migration, das heisst ihres Erscheinens an einem anderen, weit entfernten Ort, während sie selbst sich im Zustand der Versenkung oder Entraffung an ihrem gewöhnlichen Aufenthaltsort befinden. Die Migration kommt in einer zweifachen Form vor: es gibt Fälle, in denen eine Person X an dem Ort Y den Visionär des Ortes Z sieht und bei dieser Begegnung zutiefst davon überzeugt ist, dem Visionär leibhaftig begegnet zu sein (the case of Aristeas!), während es andere Fälle gibt, in denen der am Ort Z befindliche Visionär der Person X am Ort Y erscheint, die Person X aber dabei die deutliche Empfindung hat dass es sich um eine Erscheinung des am Ort Z befindlichen Visionärs handeln müsse." Also see H. Günter, *Psychologie der Legende* (Stuttgart 1960) 201.

combination of two versions of the legend.[50] In one, Aristeas dies, that is, goes into trance; in the other he is carried away with body and soul without dying, like Euthymos and Kleomedes (see Chapter Three, The Abnormal Dead). This last (hypothetical) version, however, is an unlikely source since, unlike Aristeas, Euthymos and Kleomedes do not return. Meuli thought that the legends about Aristeas lying in a trance were original and that the versions of him experiencing his adventures in the body were later rationalizations of the Greeks of Cyzicus and Proconnesus.[51] This interpretation seems more likely but misjudges the functioning of the free soul, for persons in a trance or swoon typically tell "on their return to 'life' of their experiences in the state of lethargy in the first person."[52] This identification is understandable since, as discussed above, the free soul represents the complete identity of a person. Aristeas, too, told of his adventures in the first person, just as the Siberian shamans when recounting their adventures in a trance.[53] The two versions then will have been coexistent from the very beginning. Those who knew Aristeas personally will have known that he experienced his adventures only in a trance; others who knew only his poem must have concluded that he in person had experienced his adventures.[54]

Dodds' shamanistic interpretation of the Aristeas legends induced scholars also to derive other elements of his legend from areas to the north of Greece. If these elements indeed

[50] Rohde, *Psyche* 2: 92 n. 1; also see Burkert, *Lore and Science*, 149.

[51] Meuli, *Gesammelte Schriften* 2, 857f.

[52] Hultkrantz, *Conceptions of the soul*, 284.

[53] Meuli, *Gesammelte Schriften* 2: 858; also see A. T. Hatto, *Essays on Medieval German and Other Poetry* (Cambridge 1980) 117-138, 334-338.

[54] Compare the case of Leonymos who, according to some, travelled in reality to the island of Leuke to be healed but, according to others, only did so in a dream, see Conon *FGrH* 26 F 1 § 18; Pausanias 3.19.11-13; Tertullian *De anima* 46.9; Hermias *in Phaedrum* Couvreur, p. 75.

derive from Central Asia or Siberia—areas with a strong shamanistic influence—they may be taken as at least endorsing the probability of Dodds' interpretation. But do they? Pliny told that the soul of Aristeas flew from his mouth in the shape of a raven. According to Meuli the raven-shaped soul recalled the practice of Siberian shamans.[55] Actually, Meuli could not find a direct parallel but confined himself to pointing out that in old Siberian myths the prototype of the shamans was called "Big Raven." This is not a particularly striking parallel; more important is the fact that Big Raven is a typical trickster appearing in the mythology of the northeastern Palaeo-Asiatic peoples, especially those living on the Kamschatka Peninsula and near the Bering Strait,[56] an area fairly unlikely to have influenced Greece strongly. The soul in the shape of the raven in Pliny's report clearly finds its origin in the Metapontine legend related above and, ultimately, in the close connection of Apollo with the raven.[57] The departure of the raven-shaped soul does sometimes occur elsewhere, but in all of these instances (which often have a Christian coloring) the return of the soul is

[55] Meuli, *Gesammelte Schriften* 2: 857 n. 1.

[56] See W. Bogoras, *Chuckchee Mythology* (Leiden and New York 1913) 75-83, 151-158, and *Koryak Texts* (Leiden 1917) passim; W. Yochelson, *The Koryak*, vol. 1 (Leiden and New York 1926) 274f., 289. The Big Raven figure is discussed in a number of studies by E. M. Meletinski: "Skazaniya o vorone u narodov krajnevo severa," *Revue de l'histoire de civilisation mondiale*, ser. 1, vol. 13 (1959) 86-100; "Typological Analysis of the Palaeo-Asiatic Raven Myths," *Acta ethnographica academiae scientiarum Hungaricae* 22 (1973) 107-155; E. M. Meletinski and S. N. Neklyudov (eds.), *Tipologičeskie issledovanija po folkloru* (Moscow 1975) 92-140. The two scholars to whom we owe our information, Bogoras and Yochelson, were banished to this area for political reasons during the Czarist régime, see Y. P. Alkor, "V. G. Bogoraz-Tan," *Sovetskaja Ethnografija* 1935, no. 4-5, 5-31; K. B. Shavrov, "V. I. Iochelson," ibidem, no. 2, 3-15.

[57] This is convincingly suggested by F. Williams, *Callimachus: Hymn to Apollo* (Oxford 1978) 64. For Apollo and the raven, see O. Keel, *Vögel als Boten* (Fribourg and Göttingen 1977) 79-91 and also Williams.

never reported—a fact that does not seem to have been noted and one which I am unable to explain.[58]

Andreas Alföldi links Aristeas with Central Asia. He suggests that Herodotus' gold-guarding griffins were in fact transformations of the guards of the "Golden Mountain of the Golden Heavenly Father."[59] This explanation presupposes a radical change in Aristeas' time of a tradition that, supposedly, was still found in its original form in the latter half of the last century by a German Orientalist.[60] It seems somewhat less strained—and consequently more convincing—to view Herodotus' version as a doublet replacing ants with griffins of another story of Herodotus that he learned from the Persians. In the Bactrian desert animals in the shape of ants, smaller than dogs but bigger than foxes, dig up sand containing gold when they make their burrows, gold that the Indians then steal from them in an ingenious way (Herodotus 3.102).[61]

This connection of ants and gold is confirmed by a passage in the epic *Mahābhārata* (2.48.4). When making a

[58] M. Haavio, "Der Seelenvogel," *Studia Fennica* 8 (1958) 61-86, esp. 69f.

[59] A. Alföldi, *Gnomon* 9 (1933) 567f., who is followed by Meuli, *Gesammelte Schriften* 2: 855; Dodds, *The Greeks and the Irrational*, 141; Burkert, *Lore and Science*, 162 n. 230. Similarly arbitrary is Alföldi's treatment of the Arimaspi, since he transforms one-eyed persons, seemingly chosen at random, into Arimaspi, as appears from his references to I. J. Schmidt, *Geschichte der Ost-Mongolen und ihres Fürstenhauses* (St. Petersburg 1829) 59; W. Radloff, *Proben der Volksliteratur der Türkischen Stämme Süd-Sibiriens*, vol. 1, pt. 2 (St. Petersburg 1868) 463; G. Nioradze, *Der Schamanismus bei den Sibirischen Völkern* (Stuttgart 1925) 29ff.

[60] W. Radloff, *Aus Sibirien*, 2nd ed., vol. 2 (Leipzig 1893) 6.

[61] For the "Nachleben" of this story, see G.C. Bruce, "An Account on the Μυρμηχολέων or Ant-Lion," *The Antiquaries Journal* 3 (1923) 347-364; C. Bologna (ed.), *Liber monstrorum de diversis generibus* (Milan 1977) 130; G. Cames, "Or, émeraudes et griffons," *Gazette des Beaux-Arts*, ser. 6 119 (1977) 105-108; C. Lecouteux, *De rebus in Oriente mirabilibus* (Meisenheim 1979) 72-75.

sacrifice the kings "brought the gold called Pipīlika, which is granted by the pipīlika ants, and they brought it by bucketsful and piles."[62] Similarly, in a description of a golden mountain, a Mongolian legend declares, "there is gold in nuggets which the king of the ants has piled up during his activities." Finally, this connection is made in a Tibetan chronicle where the king asks, in an enumeration of impressive works, "will I fill up Fox valley with ant-gold dust?"[63] It may eventually be shown that this ant-gold legend derived from the Altai in Siberia, although no evidence has so far been brought forward to prove this. In any case, the legend does not furnish any proof for an immediate connection between Aristeas and Central Asia. The name of the robbers, Arimaspi, a compound most likely containing the Iranian *aspa*, or "horse," also points more to the immediate neighborhood of Greece than to a connection with Central Asia.[64] A Swedish Orientalist has argued that there existed an ecstatic cult in the Iranian region whose ecstatic trances suggest a close resemblance between Zoroaster and the sha-

[62] *The Mahābhārata*, trans. and ed. J. A. van Buitenen, vol. 2 (Chicago 1975) 118.

[63] For the Mongolian legend and the Tibetan chronicle, see B. Laufer, "Die Sage von den goldgrabenden Ameisen," *T'oung Pao* 9 (1908) 429-452, reprinted in H. Walravens (ed.), *Kleinere Schriften von Berthold Laufer*, vol. 1 (Wiesbaden 1976) 1271-1294.

[64] Burkert, *Gnomon* 35 (1963) 237 n. 2; similarly Rüdiger Schmitt notes (letter Feb. 27, 1976): "Eine Deutung des Namens, die allgemein akzeptiert ist, gibt es noch nicht: Einig ist man sich nur darin, dass Herodots (4.27) Deutung als "einäugig" verfehlt sein dürfte. Alle Wahrscheinlichkeit spricht dafür, dass das Hinterglied des Kompositums iran. *aspa* 'Pferd' ist. Was sich hinter Arima-verbirgt, kann ich Ihnen leider nicht sagen; Deutungen verzeichnen etwa: Max Vasmer, *Untersuchungen über die ältesten Wohnsitze der Slaven I: Die Iranier in Südrussland* (Leipzig 1923) 12; H. H. Schaeder, *Iranica* (Berlin 1934) 17-19; Gherardo Gnoli, *Ricerche storiche sul Sīstan antico* (Rome 1967) 49 A12 (mit einer Deutung von Emile Benveniste). Beweisbar oder gar bewiesen ist keine dieser Deutungen."

mans. This view has been widely opposed and is rejected by the majority of scholars, even though, as regards soul belief, undeniable points of contact existed between Iranian and Siberian cultures.[65]

The journey of Aristeas to the Rhipaean mountains in the North also suggests an influence from the immediate neighborhood of Greece. The journey has been illuminatingly compared with Gilgamesh's trip to the "Mountain range of Mashu" (Gilgamesh 9.2.9), which was situated in the North (9.5.38).[66] In both cases the same motif is apparent: the journey to a huge mountain in the North to acquire (or receive) wisdom. Another such journey appears in the *Apocalypse of Enos*, a fragment of which occurs in the recently published *Cologne Mani Codex*: Enos is taken away by an angel to the North where he sees huge mountains and receives a revelation.[67]

The Aristeas legend then reveals the journey of the free soul in a trance but not so far any influence from shamanism. The legend of Hermotimos recounted by Apollonius also presents the free soul wandering away during a trance.[68]

---

[65] H. S. Nyberg, *Die Religionen des alten Iran*, 2nd ed. (Osnabrück 1966) 167ff.; see also M. Eliade, *Shamanism* (London 1964) 398; G. Widengren, *Die Religionen Irans* (Stuttgart 1965) 73; A. Closs, "Iranistik und Völkerkunde," *Acta Iranica* 4 (1975) 111-121. For the debate of Nyberg's views, see G. Widengren, "Henrik Samuel Nyberg and Iranian Studies in the Light of Personal Reminiscences," *Acta Iranica* 2 (1975) 419-456 and *Göttingische Gelehrte Anzeigen* 231 (1979) 54-59. For Siberia and Iran, see P. Gignoux, " 'Corps osseux et âme osseuse': essai sur le chamanisme dans l'Iran ancien," *Journal Asiatique* 267 (1979) 41-79.

[66] Burkert, *Phronesis* 14 (1969) 18f.

[67] *Cologne Mani Codex* 54:1; for the *Codex*, see A. Henrichs and L. Koenen, *ZPE* 19 (1975) 1-85, 32 (1978) 87-199, 44 (1981) 201-318, 48 (1982) 1-59. For a Greek-English version of the first half of the *Codex*, see R. Cameron and A. J. Dewey, *The Cologne Mani Codex* (Missoula, Mont. 1979). See also Bremmer, *ZPE* 39 (1980) 30.

[68] For Hermotimos, see Plutarch *Moralia* 592/3; Pliny *Natural History* 7.174; Lucian *Panegyric to the Fly* 7; Apollonius *Mirabilia* 3; Origen *Contra Celsum* 3.32; F. Graf, *Nordionische Kulte* (Rome 1983).

It seems that Hermotimos, unlike Aristeas, even practiced a certain technique of ecstasy because his murderers saw him lying naked. Changing clothing or undressing before falling into a trance is known in shamanistic séances. The shaman's garment is of the utmost importance and is even initiated with a special song, but the importance of the garment does not lie primarily in its symbolism, since the shaman also goes into trance by just winding a scarf around his head; it is the change from normal everyday dress that is the significant feature.[69] Changing clothing, however, is not restricted to shamans; Hellenistic and later mediums also practiced their art naked or lightly clad.[70] Hermotimos' ecstasy was a deep one: he was lying inert like a corpse (*sōmation*).

The burning of Hermotimos' body presupposes the belief that his soul could wander away. Similarly, in Western folktales the body was turned or the mouth covered with a cloth so that the wandering soul could not re-enter it.[71] The burning of the body is a rather ruthless way of preventing the return of the soul and rarely mentioned in Western sources; the closest parallel can be found in an Indian legend of Madras on the subject of a struggle about temple ownership. The two parties, the Jangams and the Kapus, agreed that the owners would be those who found the jasmine flower

---

[69] See U. Harva, *The Shaman Costume and its Significance* (Turku 1922); V. Diószegi, *Popular Beliefs and Folklore Traditions in Siberia* (The Hague 1968) 239-330 on the garment; V. Diószegi, *Tracing Shamans in Siberia* (Oosterhout 1968) 167-171 on the song and with a photo of a shaman with a scarf; Eliade, *Shamanism*, 146 on the significance of the change.

[70] E. Peterson, *Frühkirche, Judentum und Gnosis* (Rome, Freiburg, and Vienna 1959) 337; M. Smith, *Clement of Alexandria and a Secret Gospel of Mark* (Cambridge, Mass. 1973) 223.

[71] See L.A.J.W. Sloet, *De dieren in het Germaansche volksgeloof en volksgebruik* (The Hague 1887) 436; W. A. Craigie, *Scandinavian Folk-Lore* (London 1896) 325. These examples have to be added to those in S. Thompson, *Motif-Index of Folk-Literature*, 2nd ed. (Copenhagen 1956) E 721.1; see also Meyer-Matheis, *Vorstellung eines alter ego*, 69-71.

of the temple. To obtain this flower "the Jangams, because they were skilled in the art of transformation, decided to go, and quitting their mortal bodies went in spirit guise in search of the flower. While they were away the Kapus burnt their bodies and when the spirits returned they had nowhere to enter."[72]

Although the traditions about Hermotimos agree that his soul left the body, there is a complicating factor in that Aristotle connects Anaxagoras' theory about *nous*, or "mind," with Hermotimos: "When one man (Anaxagoras) said, then, that reason (*nous*) was present—as in animals, so throughout nature—as the cause of order and of all arrangement, he seemed like a sober man in contrast with the random talk of his predecessors. We know that Anaxagoras certainly adopted these views, but Hermotimos of Clazomenae is credited with expressing them earlier."[73] The prominence given to *nous* is not surprising in the late Archaic Age when Parmenides (B 4. 1) has exhorted "look with the *nous*," a phrase taken up by Empedocles (B 17. 21) as "gaze with the *nous*." The special use of the *nous* for inner observation in the Archaic Age is an important stage in its development that culminated in Plato's idea of the *nous* as the "eye of the soul."[74] Hermotimos, however, if we understand the

[72] A. Miles, *The Land of the Lingam* (London 1933) 132. Thompson, *Motif-Index*, E 721.2.3 s.v. Soul of the sleeper prevented from returning by burning the body, lists some other parallels, but the only real example is Hermotimos.

[73] Aristotle *Metaphysics* 984b, fragment 61 Rose, trans. W. D. Ross, *The Works of Aristotle in English Translation*, vol. 8, 2nd ed. (Oxford 1928). F. W. Carus, *Nachgelassene Werke*, vol. 4 (Leipzig 1809) 330-392 follows the tradition of this testimonium into the Byzantine Age.

[74] On the *nous* for inner observation, see W. Luther, *Archiv für Begriffsgeschichte* 10 (1966) 28f. L. Malten, *Die Sprache des menschlichen Antlitzes im frühen Griechentum* (Berlin 1961) 32-37; For Plato, see Plato *Symposium* 219 A, *Republic* 533 D, *Theaetetus* 164 A, *Sophista* 354 A; T. Gomperz, "Die Apologie der Heilkunst," *Sitzungsberichte der kaiserlichen*

rather obscure allusion of Aristotle correctly—and he is our only source—called the soul that left his body *nous*, an identification of the free soul with the ego soul (see The Ego Souls below).

Hultkrantz, too, not only repeatedly encountered this identification but could also observe that it was always—as now—the intellect within the ego soul that was identified with the free soul. As a very important cause for this identification he sees the "quality in the intellect-soul that is expressed in the phrase 'the flight of thought.' . . . Thought shows the same mobility as the free soul—or a still greater mobility. Just as dreams of distant places are interpreted as the journeys of the dream-soul to these places, so also thoughts of remote things (and especially eidetic daydreams?) sometimes imply the removal of the thought-soul to them."[75] This explanation will also suffice for Hermotimos' case—assuming at least that our interpretation of Aristotle is correct—since the Greeks too were struck by the speed of the *nous*. A simile in the *Iliad* compares the speed with which Hera goes from Ida to Olympus to the speed with which the *nous* of a much-travelled man returns to places he once visited.[76]

The Hermotimos' legend has not been connected with

Akademie der Wissenschaften in Wien, Philos.- hist. series, vol. 120, no. 9 (Vienna 1890) 166f. The expression "eye of the soul" is also found in the Pahlavi-compendium *Dēnkart* where King Vistāspa receives an ecstasy-producing drink with the name *gyān-čašm* or "eye of the soul"; see G. Widengren, *Religionsphänomenologie* (Berlin 1969) 534f., who follows the expression into the *Upanishads* and Gnostic literature.

[75] Hultkrantz, *Conceptions of the soul*, 231-233.

[76] xv.79-83; see also 7.36; *Homeric Hymn to Hermes* 43; Theognis 985; Thales 11 A 1 (Diogenes Laertius 1.35). For an interesting Anglo-Saxon example, see P. Clemoes, "*Mens absentia cogitans* in *The Seafarer* and *The Wanderer*," in D. A. Pearsall and R. A. Waldrai (eds.), *Medieval Literature and Civilisation: Studies in Memory of G. N. Garmonsway* (London 1969) 62-77.

Central Asia or Siberia and two elements seem to point to Asia Minor. The Cantharidae may have been a sneering reference to a Dionysiac organization, for after the sixth and fifth centuries Dionysos is usually represented with a cantharos in his hand, and Dionysiac cult organizations were especially common in Asia Minor.[77] On a recently published fifth-century bone graffito from Olbia the words "for Dion(ysos)" and "*psychē*" appear.[78] Moreover, in a recently excavated fifth-century grave of a woman, another so-called Orphic lamella has come to light referring to those initiated into Bacchic mysteries.[79] This evidence indicates that there was already at an early stage of the Dionysiac cult an interest in the soul and afterlife. Was the murder of Hermotimos, then, perhaps, caused by a rivalry with a Dionysiac organization also, possibly under Orphic influence, strongly interested in the soul?

The story about Hermotimos' wife is obviously an aetiological one; the exclusion of women from Eunostos' temple in Tanagra was also connected with treacherous behavior by a woman (Plutarch *Moralia* 300/1). Such an exclusion

[77] The name of Hermotimos' enemies is one of the many details that we know only from Pliny and that are due to his *curiositas*, see T. Köves-Zulauf, *Reden und Schweigen* (Munich 1972) 325ff. For the cantharos, see L. Asche, "Der Kantharos," (Diss. Univ. of Mainz 1956) 1, 18; Burkert, *Griechische Religion*, 259; the cantharos was also associated with Liber, Dionysos' Roman counterpart, see Pliny *Natural History* 33.150; Macrobius *Saturnalia* 5.21.16. For the organizations, see F. Poland, *Geschichte des griechischen Vereinswesens* (Leipzig 1909) 199.

[78] A. S. Rusyayeva, "Orphism i kult Dionisa v Olvii," *Vestnik Drevnej Istorii* 1978, no. 1, 87-104, esp. 89. The article is summarized by F. Tinnefeld, *ZPE* 38 (1980) 67-71. See also W. Burkert, "Neue Funde zur Orphik," *Informationen zum altsprachlichen Unterricht* (Steiermark, Austria) 2 (1980) 27-42, esp. 36-38; M. L. West, "The Orphics of Olbia," *ZPE* 45 (1982) 17-29.

[79] First publication: G. Foti and G. Pugliese Carratelli, *La Parola del Passato* 29 (1974) 91-126; see most recently, Burkert, above note 78; Cole, above note 21.

was not uncommon and could be found mainly on the islands and the coast of Asia Minor. We meet it in the cult of Heracles in Thasos and Miletus, Egyptian gods in Delos, Zeus and Athena Apotropaioi in Lindos, Zeus Amalos in Lindos, Poseidon in Myconos, Aphrodite Akraia in Cyprus (Strabo 14.6.3), Artemis in Ephesos where only men and free maidens were admitted (Artemidorus 4.4; Achilles Tatius 7.13), the Anakes in Elateia, and in the unknown temples of Zeus (Callimachus 1.13) and Kronos.[80] From the more reliable ethnological accounts it appears that in such a situation the women, although excluded from participation in the actual ritual, often still have, in some way, a place in the whole ritual either as actors or as spectators.[81] Our sources, however, restrict themselves to lapidary statements that do not enable us to observe whether this was also the case in ancient Greece.

Hermotimos and Aristeas are not the only figures for whom a connection has been claimed with areas influenced by shamanism. Burkert believes Abaris, to whom Heraclides Ponticus perhaps ascribed a trance journey of the soul, came from Central Asia.[82] Abaris was reputed to have come in

[80] For the complicated cult of Heracles in Thasos, see most recently B. Bergquist, *Herakles on Thasos* (Uppsala 1973); J. Pouilloux, "L'Héraklès Thasien," *Revue des études anciennes* 76 (1974 [1976]) 305-316; R. Martin, "Thasos, Quelques problèmes de structure urbaine," *Comptes Rendus de l'Académie des inscriptions et belles-lettres* 1978, 182-197; G. Roux, "L'Héracleion Thasien," *Bulletin de correspondance hellénique*, supp. 5 (1979) 191-211. For the other cults, see F. Sokolowski, *Lois sacrées de l' Asie Mineure* (Paris 1955) 114 on Miletus; Sokolowski, *Lois sacrées des cités grecques. Supplément* (Paris 1962) 56 on Delos, 88f. on Lindos; Sokolowski, *Lois sacrées des cités grecques* (Paris 1969) 82 on Elateia, 96 on Myconos; Phylarchus *FGrH* 81 F 33 on Kronos.

[81] See M. Gluckman, "The Role of the Sexes in Wiko Circumcision Ceremonies," in M. Fortes (ed.), *Social Structure: Studies presented to A. R. Radcliffe-Brown* (London 1949) 145-167; J. van Baal, *Reciprocity and the position of women* (Assen and Amsterdam 1975) 72f.

[82] For Abaris, see the very full collection of evidence by G. Moravcsik,

from the North (no nearer specification is given) with an arrow in his hand—which will have been the reason why Herodotus connected him with Apollo, who was himself an archer (Herodotus 4.36).[83] Like Aristeas, Abaris, too, presumably claimed to have travelled to the North and, in consequence, to possess higher wisdom. Dodds saw in this arrow the vehicle for his soul but there is no evidence that the Siberian shamans viewed arrows in this way.[84] The arrow as a vehicle for Abaris is found only in later testimonies,

---

"Abaris, Priester von Apollo," *Körösi CSOMA-Archivum*, suppl. 1 (1936) 104-118; Burkert, *Lore and Science*, 162; Meuli, *Gesammelte Schriften* 2: 859-864. For Heraclides and Abaris, see Bolton, *Aristeas*, 158; H. B. Gottschalk, *Heraclides of Pontus* (Oxford 1980) 121-127.

[83] On Apollo as archer, see M. P. Nilsson, *Geschichte der griechischen Religion*, 3rd ed., vol. 1 (Munich 1967) 541; L. Robert, *Hellenica* 11-12 (1960) 268-271.

[84] Dodds, *The Greeks and the Irrational*, 161 n. 34 thinks that the use of an arrow as vehicle by the soul is implicit in "the Buryat's shaman's use of arrows to summon back the souls of the sick," but this use of the arrow can instead be connected with a widespread explanation of illnesses as caused by projectiles. See L. Honko, *Krankheitsprojektile* (Helsinki 1959). When Dodds states that "it is said that the Tatar shaman's external soul is sometimes lodged in an arrow (N. K. Chadwick, *Journal of the Royal Anthropological Institute of Great Britain and Ireland* 66 [1936] 311)," he obviously infers too much from the following passage: "The object in which the soul is contained may be the sole of a shoe or a braid of horse-hair, a golden sword, or arrow, or some other small object which is kept carefully hidden away."

When Dodds, 172 n. 97, draws a parallel between Greece and India, citing as a source W. Ruben, *Acta Orientalia* 17 (1939) 164ff.—Dodds means W. Ruben, "Schamanismus im alten Indien," *Acta Orientalia* 18 (1940) 164-205—his conclusions are, in my opinion, not supported by Ruben's article. In an earlier study—"Indische und griechische Metaphysik," *Zeitschrift für Indologie und Iranistik* 8 (1931) 147-227—Ruben had already stated "ob es für die Geschichte fruchtbar sein wird, das 'Neue' in India von Nicht-indo-germanischen wie in Griechenland von Thrakern herzuleiten, mag dahingestellt bleiben (p. 152)." Eliade, *Shamanism*, 411 is also rather reserved regarding the proposed shamanistic parallel in India: "All these practices and beliefs . . . are not necessarily 'shamanistic.' "

while the earliest clearly describe him with the arrow in his hand.[85] The later version may well have been influenced by Greek traditions of flying seers, but there is no indication that arrows were associated with flying.[86]

There are many peoples who separate the role of the bow and the arrow; the Finnish national epic *Kalevala* (Runo 2.215) mentions magicians with their arrows whereas no mention is made of bows, and a detailed study of arrow symbolism in Siberia rarely mentions the bow.[87] The purpose of Abaris' arrow is unclear, but several uses are possible. Just as the plague was thought to be caused by arrows, so people believed in the healing power of arrows,[88] and Abaris was believed to have expelled the plague from those cities that had requested him to do so (Iamblichus *Life of Pythagoras* 19). Abaris also predicted the future, and Dodds himself has pointed to the use of arrows in divination, but

[85] The earliest are Herodotus 4.36; Lycurgus fragment 85 Blass; Aristotle by Iamblichus *Life of Pythagoras* 140, see Burkert, *Lore and Science*, 143 n. 127. Later testimonies are Heraclides Ponticus fragment 51c Wehrli; Iamblichus *Life of Pythagoras* 91. Meuli, *Gesammelte Schriften* 2: 858 n. 4, suggests a connection between the flying Abaris and the idea of the arrow chain, but this idea is, again, found only in the area of the Big Raven myths, see R. Pettazzoni, *Saggi di storia delle religioni e di mitologia* (Rome 1946) 63-79; G. Hatt, *Asiatic Influences in American Folklore* (Copenhagen 1949) 40-48; Eliade, *Shamanism*, 490f.

[86] See P. Wolters, "Der geflügelte Seher," *Sitzungsberichte der bayerischen Akademie der Wissenschaften*, Phil.-hist. series 1928, no. 1 (Munich 1928).

[87] N. J. Veselovskij, "Rol' strely v obrjadach i jeja semvoličeskoe značenie," *Zapiski Vostočnogo Otdelenija Russkogo Archeologičeskogo Obsčestvo* 25 (1917-1920) 273-292; B. Adler, "Pfeil und Bogen in Kult und Sage," *Der Weltkreis* 2, no. 7-8 (1931) 101-113; C. G. Seligmann, "Bow and Arrow Symbolism," *Eurasia Septentrionalis Antiqua* 9 (1934) 351-354; M. Eliade, "Notes on the Symbolism of the Arrow," in J. Neusner (ed.), *Religions in Antiquity. Essays in Memory of Erwin Ramsdell Goodenough* (Leiden 1968) 463-475.

[88] Honko, *Krankheitsprojektile*, 104-107.

this use is not restricted to shamans and was evidently known in Israel.[89] The evidence presented and the lack of parallels indicate that a connection between Abaris and Central Asia is far from certain.

Another example where a connection with shamanism has been postulated is also not above suspicion. According to Dodds, the oracle-giving head of Orpheus suggests Nordic influence; Eliade is even more certain and considers it a clear shamanistic detail.[90] A similar use of the severed head is, however, also testified for the Celts, Icelanders, and many other peoples.[91] The wide occurrence of this motif does not

[89] Lycurgus fragment 85 Blass; Apollonius *Mirabilia* 4; Scholia on Aristophanes *Equites* 729; Suidas s.v. *Abaris*; Dodds, *The Greeks and the Irrational*, 141 n. 34. For instances in Israel, see II *Kings* 13, 15-19; S. Tury, "New Evidence for Belomancy in Ancient Palestine and Syria," *Journal of the American Oriental Society* 81 (1961) 27-34; F. M. Cross, Jr., *Eretz Israel* 8 (1967) p. 13* n. 33; G. J. Botterweck and H. Ringgren (eds.), *Theologisches Wörterbuch zum Alten Testament*, vol. 3 (Stuttgart 1978) 133. Also see M. Räsänen, "Wahrsagung und Verlosung mit Pfeil und Bogen," in *Symbolae in honorem Z. V. Togan* (Istanbul 1950-1955) 273-277. In *Ezekiel* 21.21 it is said: "For the king of Babylon stood at the parting of the way, at the head of the two ways, to use divination: he made his arrows bright." W. Zimmerli, *Ezechiël*, vol. 1 (Neukirchen-Vluyn, Germany 1969) 489 points out, however, that our Babylonian sources do not mention such a divinatory practice. For the use of arrows in Arabic divination, see J. Wellhausen, *Reste arabischen Heidentums*, 2nd ed. (Berlin and Leipzig 1897) 132f.

[90] Dodds, *The Greeks and the Irrational*, 147; Eliade, *Shamanism*, 391. For Orpheus, see W. Burkert, *Homo necans*, RGVV, vol. 32 (Berlin and New York 1972) 224f.; E. R. Panyagna, "Catálogo de representaciones de Orfeo en el arte antiguo," pt. 1, *Helmantica* 23 (1973) 83-135, esp. cat. no. 75-76, 93(?), 95; pt. 2, ibidem, 393-416, esp. cat. no. 107-111; F. Graf, *Eleusis und die orphische Dichtung Athens in vorhellenistischer Zeit*, RGVV, vol. 33 (Berlin and New York 1974) 11f. For other Greek examples, see L. Brisson, "Aspects politiques de la bisexualité," in M. B. de Boer and T. A. Edridge (eds.), *Hommages à Maarten J. Vermaseren*, vol. 1 (Leiden 1978) 80-122; J.-D. Gauger, "Phlegon von Tralleis, mirab. III," *Chiron* 10 (1980) 225-261.

[91] For the Celts, see A. Reinach, "Les têtes coupées et les trophées en Gaule," *Revue Celtique* 34 (1913) 38-60, 253-286 and "Le rite des têtes

of course preclude with certainty a shamanistic derivation of the Orpheus myth, but it does not increase the probability of this suggestion. We conclude that no convincing evidence exists for shamanistic influence on Archaic Greece; when there are parallels, such as the identification of death and trance, changing clothing before trance, and the oracle-giving head, these are not exclusively shamanistic. It has not yet even been shown that the Scythians who were supposed by Dodds to have influenced the Greeks knew a shamanistic journey of the soul![92]

Where does this leave us with Aristeas and Hermotimos? According to Dodds, the tale of Hermotimos is an example of the influence of shamanism in Greece at the end of the Archaic Age. Before Dodds Karl Meuli claimed the same influence on the legend of Aristeas.[93] These interpretations have been accepted by, amongst others, Walter Burkert and, understandably, Mircea Eliade since they complement

---

coupées chez les Celtes," *Revue de l'histoire des religions* 67 (1913) 41-48; G. L. Kittredge, *A Study of Gawain and the Green Knight* (Cambridge, Mass. 1916) 177-184; P. Lambrechts, *L'exaltation de la tête dans la pensée et dans l'art des Celtes* (Bruges 1954); A. Ross, "The human head in insular pagan Celtic religion, "*Proceedings of the Society of Antiquaries of Scotland* 91 (1960) 10-43, esp. 39f. For Iceland the case of Mímir is well known, see *Ynglinga saga* c. 4.7; *Eyrbyggja saga* c. 43; E. Mogk, *Novellistische Darstellung mythologischer Stoffe Snorris und seiner Schule* (Helsinki 1923) 22; H. Naumann and I. Naumann, *Isländische Volksmärchen* (Jena 1923) 25. For other peoples, see Burkert, *Homo necans*, 224 n. 30; A. Dickson, "Valentine and Orson" (Diss. Columbia University, New York 1929) 200-216; W. Klingbeil, *Kopf- und Maskenzauber in der Vorgeschichte und bei den Primitiven* (Diss. Univ. of Bonn 1932) 96-107; L. Petzoldt, *Der Tote als Gast* (Helsinki 1968) 56-59; A. von Avanzin, "Bemerkungen zum weissagenden Totenkopf," *Carinthia*, 1st ser., 160 (1970) 974-977; L. Kretzenbacher, "Zur Kärntner Sage vom redenden Totenkopf," ibidem 162 (1972) 499-503.

[92] Dodds, *The Greeks and the Irrational*, 140; compare Eliade, *Shamanism*, 395; K. Dowden, *Revue des études grecques* 93 (1980) 486-492.

[93] Dodds, *The Greeks and the Irrational*, 141-144; Meuli, *Gesammelte Schriften* 2: 853-859.

Eliade's interpretation of shamanism as an archaic technique of ecstasy.[94] Yet his interpretation has recently been unanimously rejected by those scholars who have sought a more detailed definition of the shamanistic complex. Despite mutual differences they all agree that the shaman is a phenomenon restricted in time, place, appearance, and activities. Ecstasy and the journey of the soul occur in too many places to be distinguishing traits.[95]

As shown above, the souls of Aristeas and Hermotimos could wander away in a trance. Such ecstatic journeys presuppose a free soul able to leave the body. Now it appears probable that *psyche* sufficiently corresponds with the notion of the free soul as defined by Arbman and his pupils to be accepted as the Greek version of the free soul. Consequently, it seems acceptable to claim also the memorates of Aristeas and Hermotimos as valid evidence for Greek soul belief. Finally, although shamanism did not influence the development of the Greek free soul, it, as Burkert remarks, "has in any case performed the useful function of taking the so-called (shamanistic) myths and legends seriously and showing how they make sense as clues to actual cult practices."[96]

In addition to the legends of Aristeas, Hermotimos, and

[94] Burkert, *Lore and Science*, 162-166, who, however, recently has become more skeptical, see the "Preface to the English Edition"; Eliade, *Shamanism*, 389 and *Zalmoxis, the Vanishing God* (Chicago 1972) 37.

[95] D. Schröder, "Zur Struktur des Schamanismus," *Anthropos* 50 (1955) 849-881, reprinted in C. A. Schmitz (ed.), *Religions-Ethnologie* (Frankfurt on Main 1964) 296-334; L. Vajda, "Zur phaseologischen Stellung des Schamanismus," *Ural-altaische Jahrbücher* 31 (1959) 455-485, reprinted in Schmitz, ibidem, 265-295; I. Paulson, "Zur Phänomenologie des Schamanismus," *Zeitschrift für Religions- und Geistesgeschichte* 16 (1964) 121-141; E. Lot-Falck, "Le chamanisme en Sibérie: essai de mise au point," *Asie du Sud-Est et Monde Insulindien* 4, no. 3 (1973) 1-10; Hultkrantz, "A Definition of Shamanism," *Temenos* 9 (1973) 25-37 and "Ecological and Phenomenological Aspects of Shamanism," in L. Bäckman and Å. Hultkrantz (eds.), *Studies in Lapp Shamanism* (Stockholm 1978) 9-35.

[96] Burkert, *Lore and Science*, 165.

Abaris, other reports exist about a journey of the soul. Heraclides Ponticus most likely mentioned a journey of the soul in a description of the miracle worker Empedocles resurrecting a woman who had been in a coma for many days.[97] He also ascribed a journey of the soul to a certain Empedotimos, but Rohde saw that Empedotimos was only a fictitious character in a dialogue of Heraclides, and it seems nearly certain that his name was a composition of Empedocles and Hermotimos.[98] Unfortunately, we cannot be too sure of the story of Empedocles either, since "it is clear that any evidence about anything that can be traced to the authority of Heraclides must be treated with the greatest reserve. It is also clear that it cannot be peremptorily dismissed as sheer invention, for the elements out of which he moulded his fancies were often provided by earlier literature or tradition."[99] Since there is no other information regarding Empedocles, the authenticity of Heraclides' report must remain in doubt.

The young Aristotle seems to have displayed a special interest in the activity of the soul.[100] He wrote a dialogue, *Eudemos*, also known as *On the Soul*, in which he, as an Arabic source informs us, tells "of the Greek king whose soul was caught up in ecstasy" while his body remained inanimate. We are not informed which king it was, but it can hardly have been a contemporary one, and the whole episode looks rather like fiction.[101]

[97] Heraclides Ponticus fragments 76-89 Wehrli.

[98] Heraclides fragment 93 Wehrli. For Empedotimos' name, see Rohde, *Psyche* 2: 95; but also compare Burkert, *Lore and Science*, 366 n. 89, and Gottschalk, *Heraclides of Pontus*, 111 n. 79.

[99] Bolton, *Aristeas*, 174.

[100] For a discussion of Aristotle's ideas about the soul, see H. Wijsenbeek-Wijler, *Aristotle's Concept of the Soul, Sleep and Dreams* (Diss. Univ. of Amsterdam 1976).

[101] See W. D. Ross, *The Works of Aristotle in English Translation*, vol. 12 (Oxford 1952) 23; R. Walzer, *Greek into Arabic* (Oxford 1962) 38-47, who ascribes the fragment to the *Eudemos* (42f.).

Aristotle also attended, as his pupil Clearchus relates, a psychic experiment in which someone with "a wand which draws the soul out of the body," a *psychoulkos rhabdos*, experimented on a sleeping boy:

For after having struck the boy with his wand, he pulled out the soul and, so to speak, leading the soul with the wand far from the body, he showed that the body was motionless and, completely unhurt, did not feel the blows of those who mangled him, like a body bereaved of its soul. Since the soul, in the meantime, had carried itself far away from the body, the man touched the child again with his wand and, after the return of the soul, it told everything that had happened. That is why both the spectators of this impressive experiment and Aristotle himself believed that the soul is separable from the body.[102]

This is a very interesting account but it is unfortunately, as many critics have pointed out, pure fiction.[103]

This sometimes neglected evidence has rightly been compared with the legends about Hermotimos and Aristeas.[104]

[102] Clearchus fragment 7 Wehrli. For boys as mediums, see T. Hopfner, "Die Kindermedien in den griechisch-ägyptischen Zauberpapyri," in *Receuil N. P. Kondakov* (Prague 1926) 65-74; A.-J. Festugière, *La révélation d'Hermès Trismégiste*, vol. 1 (Paris 1944) 348-350; Peterson, *Frühkirche, Judentum und Gnosis*, 339; C. Blacker, *The Catalpa Bow. A Study of Shamanistic Practices in Japan* (London 1975) 254, 300, 347 on modern Japan. The explanation of E. R. Dodds, *The Ancient Concept of Progress* (Oxford 1973) 190 leaves the preference for boys unexplained. For the wand, see F.J.M. de Waele, *The Magic Staff or Rod* (Diss. Univ. of Nijmegen 1927); Peterson, *Frühkirche, Judentum und Gnosis*, 260, but the subject is in need of a new analysis. The connection with the Tree of Life or Cosmic Tree seems to be important, see G. Widengren, *The King and the Tree of Life in Ancient Near Eastern Religion* (Uppsala 1951) 20-41; J. L. Melena, "En torno al σκῆπτρον homérico," *Cuadernos de Filología clásica* 3 (1972) 321-356; J. Gonda, *Selected Studies*, vol. 4 (Leiden 1975) 160-170.

[103] U. von Wilamowitz-Moellendorff, *Der Glaube der Hellenen*, vol. 2 (Berlin 1932) 253; M. Hengel, *Judentum und Hellenismus*, 2nd ed. (Tübingen 1973) 200 n. 2; G.J.D. Aalders, *Pilatus en Herodes* (Kampen 1975) 20 n. 32.

[104] M. Detienne, "De la catalepsie à l'immortalité de l'âme," *La nouvelle Clio* 10-12 (1958-1962) 123-135.

However, Hermotimos could fall into a trance on his own, whereas the boy seems to have been hypnotized. But here again, even though the authenticity of these accounts is highly suspect, they could hardly have originated without the former existence of the concept of the free soul.

Dodds began his "shamanistic" interpretation of the legends of Aristeas and Hermotimos with an analysis of the fragment of Pindar cited in Chapter One. In it Pindar says that although the body sleeps, an image of life remains that reveals the coming of adversities or joys. As Dodds observed, Xenophon describes the same behavior of the soul during sleep: "It is in sleep that it enjoys a certain insight into the future; and this apparently, because it is freest in sleep" (Xenophon *Cyropaedy* 8.7.21, tr. Dodds). Dodds also suggested that this behavior of the soul during sleep can probably also be found in the *Eumenides* (104) of Aeschylus where Clytemnestra says "for in sleep the *phrēn* (the mind) is lightened with eyes (see The Ego Souls below).[105] It seems that here, as in the case of Hermotimos, the intellectual soul has been identified with the free soul.

Hippocrates gives a much more interesting description of the soul's behavior during sleep: "But when the body is at rest the soul (*psychē*), being set in motion and awake, administers her own household and of herself performs all the acts of the body. For the body when asleep has no perception; but the soul when awake has cognizance of all things—sees what is visible, hears what is audible, walks, touches, feels pain, ponders. In a word, all the functions of body and soul are performed by the soul during sleep."[106] This passage finely illustrates a typical feature of the free soul absent in Homer: the soul becomes active as soon as

[105] Dodds, *The Greeks and the Irrational*, 135, 157 n. 3. Dodds also compares Plato *Republic* 571 D and Aristotle fragment 10 Rose.

[106] Hippocrates *De victus ratione* 4.86, trans. W.H.S. Jones, *Hippocrates*, vol. 4 (London and Cambridge, Mass. 1931) 421-423.

the body sleeps. Here, the soul also completely takes over the activities of the individual.

Dodds remarked that in the passages of Pindar and Xenophon, " 'psychic' and bodily activity vary inversely: the *psychē* is most active when the body is asleep or, as Aristotle added, when it lies at the point of death."[107] Dodds also noted a similar pattern of behavior for the soul in the cases of Aristeas and Hermotimos. These observations mean that in fact Dodds had already identified the typical behavior of the free soul, for as explained in Chapter One, the free soul becomes active during unconsciousness and at the moment of death. Since Arbman's investigations had evidently escaped him and he understandably felt unable to explain this pattern of behavior from the Greek tradition, Dodds linked them to shamanistic practices. This would mean that these typical features of the "primitive" concept of the soul had already disappeared from the whole of Greece at a very early stage of Greek civilization and suddenly reappeared in post-Homeric times for some obscure reason. As shown above, this shamanistic interpretation is based on inadequate parallels. When we take into account that the dualistic concept of the soul at one time seems to have existed almost everywhere, including among Indo-European peoples, it is much less complicated to suppose both that the features of *psychē* found in Pindar and Hippocrates did not occur in the epic tradition because there only "message" dreams are found and that the absence of descriptions of a journey of the soul in the epic was due to the subject matter of those poems.

---

[107] Dodds, *The Greeks and the Irrational*, 140; compare Burkert, *Griechische Religion*, 446: "Zunächst ist dieses beständiges Etwas (i.e. the soul) keineswegs identisch mit dem empirischen Wachbewusstsein; *Pindar beschreibt es geradezu in Antithese zu diesem*: es schläft, wenn die Glieder tätig sind, es zeigt sein Wesen allenfalls im Traum, und dann im Tod" (my italics).

Thus the passages from Pindar, Hippocrates, and Xenophon like the legends of Aristeas and Hermotimos exemplify the existence of the concept of the free soul in the Archaic Age.

The Ego Souls

In his analysis of the dualistic nature of the soul Arbman distinguished between the free soul and the body souls. The body souls are active during the waking life of the living individual. Arbman found that the body souls are usually divided into two parts: the life soul, often identified with the breath, and the ego soul. The breath soul has been linked in this chapter to the development of the free soul in Archaic Age Greece; the ego soul, however, as it appears in Greece during the Archaic Age, is richer and more varied than the descriptions offered by Arbman and his pupils. Arbman, who was clearly more interested in the free soul, to a certain extent neglected the ego soul, but this neglect was not his alone; his contemporaries and predecessors too were more interested in the problems of afterlife than in those of psychology and, consequently, did not furnish the data Arbman could have used. This is especially true in the studies of soul belief in North Eurasia and Oceania that are based on very fragmentary and scattered sources.[108]

Arbman used the ego soul to denote individual living consciousness in contrast to the free soul and the life soul, but he did not describe the varied psychological aspects of the soul linked to the individual in the Greek Archaic Age. Hultkrantz was more aware of the multiple psychological aspects of the ego soul and his identification of multiple ego souls and his definition of them as "potencies behind the various

[108] See Paulson, *Die primitiven Seelenvorstellungen*, 254; Fischer, *Studien über Seelenvorstellungen*, 321.

acts and phases of the life of consciousness" are apt.[109] Yet his descriptions do not suggest the psychological richness and variety of the Greek concepts. In the epic tradition the major parts of the Greek ego soul were the *thymos, noos*, and *menos*.[110] In the course of the Archaic Age *psyche* incorporated the psychological attributes of *thymos*. In the case of Hermotimos, the *noos* was associated with the free soul but this particular form of the development toward the unitary soul remained unique.

The most frequently occurring form for the ego soul in the Homeric epic is *thymos*.[111] Unlike *psyche, thymos* is active only when the body is awake. *Thymos* can urge people on. For example, when Achilles is causing havoc among the Trojans and is going to meet Aeneas "his brave *thymos* roused him" (xx.174). Sometimes *thymos* expresses hope, but it is always the hope to act, not to receive something. After Patroclus had been killed, it is said of the Trojans that "their *thymos* strongly hoped to pull away Patroclus' body from under Ajax" (xvii.234). *Thymos* is, above all, the source of emotions. Friendship and feelings of revenge, joy and grief, anger and fear—all spring from *thymos*. Deiphobus "feared in his *thymos* the spear of the fiery Meriones" (xiii.163); Hector reproaches Paris when he does not join

[109] Hultkrantz, *Conceptions of the soul*, 220.

[110] We restrict ourselves to the epic since in the post-Homeric times the content of the ego soul is already affected by the development toward a unitary soul; see the literature quoted in note 29.

[111] Böhme, *Die Seele und das Ich*, 19-23; Onians, *The Origins of European Thought*, 23-69; B. Snell, *Die Entdeckung des Geistes*, 4th ed. (Göttingen 1975) 19-22; Harrison, "Notes," 65-72; Verdenius, "Archaische denkpatronen 3," 100f.; J. P. Lynch and G. B. Miles, "In search of *Thumos*: Toward an understanding of a Greek psychological term," *Prudentia* 17 (1980) 3-9; S. Darcus Sullivan, "How a Person relates to θυμός in Homer," *Indogermanische Forschungen* 85 (1980) and "The Function of θυμός in Hesiod and the Greek Lyric Poets," *Glotta* 59 (1981) 147-155; A. Cheyns, "Θυμός dans Homère, *Iliade*, VII.67-218," *L'Antiquité classique* 50 (1981) 137-147; Claus, *Toward the Soul*, 21f.

the battle: "Fool, wrongly you stored up bitter anger in your *thymos*" (vi.326). When Hector has challenged the Greeks, Menelaos finally stands up and "complained loudly in his *thymos*" (vii.95). However, the action of *thymos* is not always restricted to emotion. Sometimes it serves intellectual ends. Yet, these are not the intellectual activities of an armchair scholar.[112] Deliberations take place in difficult situations, in an atmosphere charged with emotions. When Odysseus is left alone by the Greeks in a battle, "he spoke to his proud *thymos*" (xi.403). Having realized the two possibilities left to him, he ends his deliberations by asking, "but why does my *thymos* consider that?" (xi.407).

The *thymos* was thought to reside mainly in the chest (iv.152 etc.), where its principal seat was the *phrenes* (see below). Hera asks Poseidon: "Does not the *thymos* in your *phrenes* feel pity for the dying Trojans?" (viii.202). In a few cases the *thymos* is associated with the limbs. When Odysseus meets his mother Antikleia in the Land of the Ghosts, she reproaches him by saying that it was yearning for him that killed her, and not an "illness which especially takes away the *thymos* from the limbs by its hateful wasting away" (11.201). This association with the limbs does not contradict its normal location, for Antikleia stressed in this way the effect of the *thymos* upon a healthy body.

The *thymos* normally stays in its place and does not move around, but it is affected by a swoon. Homer, as we have already seen in the previous section, describes all swoons according to a set pattern. This pattern indicates that upon awakening from a swoon, the *thymos* resumes its interrupted activity. After Andromache has fainted at the sight of Hector's body being dragged around the city, her recovery is described thus: "And when she had recovered her breath and the *thymos* was concentrated into her *phrēn*, she said

[112] H. Diller, *Kleine Schriften zur antiken Literatur* (Munich 1971) 364.

. . ." (XXII.475). These words suggest that during a swoon the *thymos* leaves its original seat, but they do not necessarily imply that it always leaves the body, as has been suggested.[113] The verb used, *ageirō* "to collect," or "to gather," could point to a concentration of something that has been dispersed in the body. This is suggested in another passage: when Menelaos realizes that he is not dangerously hit, "the *thymos* became again concentrated in [not: into] his chest" (IV.152).[114] The description of Sarpedon's swoon, however, seems to indicate an actual leaving of the body since the wind is said "to restore to life him who had blown forth his *thymos*" (V.697f.).[115] Not only does it seem that the *thymos* was sometimes represented as a kind of breath, but the concept could also have been influenced by the concept of *psychē*.

What was the *thymos* originally? It has recently been shown that the *thymos* must once have been a substance that could be brought into movement, and this observation again lends support to an old etymology connecting *thymos* with words such as the Latin *fumus*, or "smoke."[116] *Thymos* is indeed sometimes represented as a kind of breath (IV.524; XVI.468), but an identification with the *psychē* should not be assumed from this one point of resemblance.[117]

More intellectual is *noos*, which after Homer usually is

[113] Against Otto, *Die Manen*, 28; Verdenius, "Archaische denkpatronen 2," 112 n. 67.

[114] Böhme, *Die Seele und das Ich*, 101; Schnaufer, *Frühgriechischer Totenglaube*, 196f.

[115] However, the precise meaning of these lines is debated, see Verdenius, "Archaische denkpatronen 2," 112 n. 67.

[116] See H. Rix, *Indogermanische Forschungen* 70 (1965) 38; Frisk, *Griechisches etymologisches Wörterbuch*, and Chantraine, *Dictionnaire étymologique*, s.v. *thymos*; G. Drosdowski, in R. Schmitt (ed.), *Etymologie* (Darmstadt 1977) 208f. Onians, *The Origins of European Thought*, 47 suggests that originally *thymos* was the vapor arising from warm blood.

[117] Against E. Bickel, *Homerischer Seelenglaube* (Berlin 1925) 266f.

written in its contracted form as *nous*[118] It is the mind or an act of mind, a thought or a purpose. Whatever Patroclus may do, "the *noos* of Zeus is always more powerful than that of men" (XVI.688); Nausicaä "laid the lash on her mules with *noos*" (6.320), so that her maids and Odysseus could follow her on foot; Zeus reproaches Athena: "Did you not yourself devise that *noos*?" (5.23). Yet the *noos* is not exclusively intellectual. Agamemnon "rejoiced in his *noos*" (8.78); Paris says of Hector that "the *noos* in his chest is fearless" (III.63). The intellectual meaning is, however, much more prominent.

The *noos* is always located in the chest (IV.309 etc.) but it is never conceived of as something material. It cannot be struck or pierced or blown out. There is nothing that even hints at an origin as an organ of the body. Many attempts have been made to etymologize *noos*, but until the present day none of these has gained general acceptance. The most recent attempts agree in suggesting a connection between *noos* and *neomai*, "to return," but they differ sharply in the explanations of the semantic developments, and a definitive solution does not yet seem to be forthcoming.[119]

Like *noos*, *menos* is not a physical organ.[120] It is a mo-

[118] Böhme, *Die Seele und das Ich*, 52-63; Snell, *Entdeckung des Geistes*, 21-24; Harrison, "Notes," 72-74; K. von Fritz, "Νόος and νοεῖν in the Homeric Poems," *Classical Philology* 38 (1943) 79-93; Verdenius, "Archaische denkpatronen 3," 106f.; S. Darcus, "How a Person relates to νόος in Homer and the Greek Lyric Poets," *Glotta* 58 (1980) 33-44; Claus, *Toward the Soul*, 19-21.

[119] See C. J. Ruijgh, *Etudes sur la grammaire et le vocabulaire du grec mycénien* (Amsterdam 1967) 370f.; E. Risch, *Wortbildung der homerischen Sprache*, 2nd ed. (Berlin and New York 1974) 8f.; Ruijgh, *Mnemosyne*, 4th ser. 29 (1976) 314f.; D. Frame, *Myth of Return in Early Greek Epic* (New Haven and London 1978).

[120] Onians, *The Origins of European Thought*, 52f.; R. Schmitt, *Dichtung und Dichtersprache in indogermanischer Zeit* (Wiesbaden 1967) 103-121; Verdenius, "Archaische denkpatronen 3," 103; G. Nagy, *Comparative Studies*

mentary impulse of one, several, or even all mental and physical organs largely directed toward a specific activity. This impulse, although observed by the subject, can only be influenced by him to a limited extent.[121] When Odysseus' father Laertes rejoiced in the fight against the suitors, "Pallas Athene breathed a great *menos* into him . . . and whirling back he swung his long-shafted spear" (24.520); after the wounded Glaucus has prayed to Apollo, the god "immediately eased his pains . . . and put *menos* into his *thymos*" (XVI.529); when Nestor tries to resolve the dispute between Achilles and Agamemnon, he appeals to the king: "Son of Atreus, stop your *menos*" (I.282).

Menos can also be the fury of a warrior. In the heat of the battle Helenus sketches to Aeneas and Hector the desperate situation caused by Diomedes, for "he rages furiously and no man can match him with his *menos*" (VI.101). Georges Dumézil has suggested that the Homeric *menos* was similar to the Irish *dasâcht* and the Germanic *Wut*, the martial rage that made the warrior behave in the same way as Odin's men: "his men rushed forwards without armor, were as mad as dogs or wolves, bit their shields, and were strong as bears or wild bulls, and killed people at a blow, but neither fire nor iron told upon themselves. This was called the Berserk fury."[122]

---

in *Greek and Indic Meter* (Cambridge, Mass. 1974) 265-269; Claus, *Toward the Soul*, 24f.

[121] R. Schröter, "Die Aristie als Grundform homerischer Dichtung und der Freiermord in der Odyssee," (Diss. Univ. of Marburg 1950) 47.

[122] G. Dumézil, *Horace et les Curiaces* (Paris 1942) 21-23. Also compare the behavior of the young Swiss mercenaries in the Middle Ages: H. G. Wackernagel, *Altes Volkstum der Schweiz* (Basel 1956) passim. For a shamanistic initiatory fury, see E. Lot-Falck, "Les incarnations de l'ilbis Yakoute," in I. Melikoff (ed.), *Traditions religieuses et parareligieuses des peuples altaïques* (Paris 1972) 65-77. For the Berserks, see *Ynglinga saga* 6, in Snorri Sturluson, *Heimskringla*, trans. S. Laing, 1st ed. 1844 (London

Although *menos* is indeed used to denote the ardor of the warrior, in Homer the equivalent of the berserk's fury is expressed by the word *lyssa*, or "wolf's rage," as appears from the words of Odysseus when he describes Hector: "Hector, exulting greatly in his might, rages vehemently, relying on Zeus and holding no one in respect, neither men nor gods. And the powerful *lyssa* has entered him" (ix.237-9, tr. Lincoln).[123] A warrior possessed by the *lyssa* had lost control over himself and he had stopped being fully human: *daimoni isos*, or "resembling a supernatural being," is the normal term for a warrior gone berserk.[124] Yet, the *menos* on the battlefield can hardly have been negligible either, since the existence of the words *dusmenēs* and Persian *dusmanah* (equivalent to the Turkish *düsman*), or "enemy," suggests that the enemies were especially feared because of their adverse *menos*. The *menos* was located either in the chest (xix.202) or in the *thymos* (xvi.529). It could also be located in the *phrenes* (1.89).

It has been argued that *menos* was conceived as something gaseous, since the Abantes are described as "breathing forth *menos*" (ii.536), and during a nightly raid "the owl-eyed Athena breathed *menos* into Diomedes" (x.482).[125] However, the last example can be compared to expressions from the Veda where it is said that thought, skill, and spiritual power are breathed toward someone without any suggestion that they are gaseous by nature. The origin of this

1961) 11; O. Höfler, in H. Beck et al. (eds.), *Reallexikon der germanischen Altertumskunde*, vol. 2 (Berlin and New York 1976) 298-304.

[123] B. Lincoln, "Homeric λύσσα: 'Wolfish Rage,'" *Indogermanische Forschungen* 80 (1975) 98-105. For Hector's *lyssa*, see J. Redfield, *Nature and Culture in the Iliad* (Chicago and London 1975) 201f.

[124] M. Daraki, "Le héros à *menos* et le héros *daimoni isos*. Une polarité homérique?" *Annali della Scuola normale superiore di Pisa*, 3rd ser. 10 (1980) 1-24.

[125] Onians, *The Origins of European Thought*, 52.

expression, which derives from a common Indo-European *langage poétique*, can be explained from a quality of breathing. Just as one breathes into the fire and fans it, so one breathes into persons spiritual powers and fans them.[126] This suggestion finds support in Greek expressions where it is said that *menos* is difficult to "put out" (xvi.621), or that *menos* is "inextinguishable" (xxii.96). However, the expression "breathing forth *menos*" most likely finds its origin in the meaning of *menos* as martial rage: the heavy breathing shows the energy spent in battle.

Finally, it may be observed that *menos* has not developed in the same direction as the related Indian *manas* and Persian *manah*. The latter two both expanded into a secondary free soul,[127] while *menos* occupies only a small place in the Greek ego soul. The reasons for this separate development still have to be investigated.

How do these ego souls compare with Hultkrantz's conception of the ego soul? Hultkrantz, who has studied the ego soul in the most detailed way, defines it as

a body-soul of a rather heterogeneous and sometimes obscure nature. In its "pure" form it constitutes a hypostasis of the stream of consciousness, the centre for thinking, willing and feeling—the mind in a wide sense. But at the same time as in this way the ego-soul shows its close kinship with our concept of the ego, it manifests certain peculiar features which makes it clear that it is not an expression for the individual's own personality, but a being within the individual which endows him with thought and will etc. The soul of consciousness has probably obtained its function of potency in the individual on the same grounds as the life-soul: the perceptions, thoughts, desires etc. which constitute the conscious content of the ego often manifest a certain independence, especially when (as in above all psychasthenic persons) in con-

---

[126] P. Thieme, "Die Wurzel Vat," in *Asiatica. Festschrift Friedrich Weller* (Leipzig 1954) 656-666.

[127] Paulson, *Die primitiven Seelenvorstellungen*, 363-365.

sequence of their strength they are found to conflict with other tendencies in the mind or acquire the character of compulsive notions, compulsive acts, phobias and so forth. This peculiarity of the ego-soul explains why we find it now split into several potencies, now taking up an exaggeratedly independent, at times superior attitude towards its owner.[128]

It is clear that there are many points of resemblance to the *thymos, noos,* and *menos,* but Hultkrantz's definition does not suggest the richness and variety of the Greek material. Also, Hultkrantz's own material does not correspond completely with his definition, since his "pure" form is evidently an abstraction nowhere encountered in reality. Every tribe he studied appears to have had its own variants.[129]

In addition to *thymos, noos,* and *menos* there are a number of organs with both physical and psychological attributes. These organs may be called rudimentary ego potencies.[130] The gradual disappearance of the physical associations of these terms seems to have led to the greater development of the ego soul.[131] The most important of these are the *phrenes,* the location of the emotions of joy and grief, fear and anger.[132] The *phrenes* also have an intellectual attribute partially overlapping with *noos* but different "in that *noos* is more concerned with noticing present facts or picturing future ones, *phrenes* with reasoning about them."[133] When

[128] Hultkrantz, *Conceptions of the soul,* 208f.

[129] Hultkrantz, *Conceptions of the soul,* 209-241; similarly, Paulson, *Die primitiven Seelenvorstellungen,* 253-265.

[130] See Paulson, *Die primitiven Seelenvorstellungen,* 255.

[131] See the material collected by Y. H. Toivonen, "Spuren primitiven Seelenvorstellungen in der Sprache," *Finnisch-ugrische Forschungen* 27 (1941) 205-224.

[132] Böhme, *Die Seele und das Ich,* 37-52; Onians, *The Origins of European Thought,* 13-30; B. Snell, *Der Weg zum Denken und zur Wahrheit* (Göttingen 1978) 53-90; S. Darcus, "A Person's Relation to φρήν in Homer, Hesiod and the Lyric Poets," *Glotta* 57 (1979) 159-173; Claus, *Toward the Soul,* 16-21.

[133] A.W.H. Adkins, *From the Many to the One* (London 1970) 20.

Menelaos wanted to take Adrastos prisoner, Agamemnon strongly objected and "he persuaded the *phrenes* of his brother" (VI.61); Agamemnon is described in the prologue of the *Doloneia* as "pondering many things in his *phrenes*" (X.4).

Scholars used to suppose that the *phrenes* meant the diaphragm, but strong arguments can be made that Homer must also have meant the lungs.[134] It is certain, however, that later on the *phrenes* were understood as the diaphragm, although this meaning does not seem to fit everywhere.[135] The different location has baffled scholars, but can perhaps be understood if we look to the breath as common factor in emotions such as joy and grief and in organs such as the lungs and the diaphragm. When we feel good, *euphrōn*, or "with a good *phrēn*, cheerful," our breath stays even, but feelings of anxiety or unrest change our normal way of breathing to panting, for example; in such a case we feel the breath near our diaphragm. The Greeks would have learned the connection of the breath with the lungs early on through their many sacrifices and through injuries on the battlefield.

The *prapides* are of far less importance; they are the seat of intelligence (I.608), desire (XXIV.514), and grief (X.43). Their exact location is unclear, but they have been explained as being the lungs.[136]

In a number of passages Homer uses the word *cholos*, or "gall," for wrath.[137] The physical attribute usually dominates as in the following outburst of Achilles when he quotes the words of his own Myrmidons: "Hard son of Peleus, your

---

[134] Onians, *The Origins of European Thought*, 13-30; Verdenius, "Archaische denkpatronen 3," 101.

[135] S. Ireland and F.L.D. Steel, "Φρένες as an Anatomical Organ in the Works of Homer," *Glotta* 53 (1975) 183-194.

[136] Onians, *The Origins of European Thought*, 29, 30, 38.

[137] Verdenius, "Archaische denkpatronen 3," 103f.

mother reared you on *cholos*" (xvi.203). The psychological aspect is prominent in vi.335 where Paris says to Hector that he did not sit down "from *cholos* against the Trojans."

Finally, there are *kardia*, *kēr*, or "heart," and *ētor* that is usually translated to mean "heart" but that originally might have meant "vein."[138] These words denote a whole spectrum of feelings, like *thymos*, but do not have an intellectual content and are rarely the seat of desire or hope. When Aias has rebuked Achilles, he answers him: "my *kardia* swells with *cholos*" (ix.646); the Greeks buried their dead in silence, "mourning in their *kēr*" (vii.428); Odysseus' "*ētor* quivered with eagerness" (v.670).

Kēr seems to be evolving away from its physical origin, the reason perhaps why *kardia* was formed, which is never located in another place. Hector tells Paris: "my *kēr* is mourning in my *thymos*" (vi.523f.); Alkinoos answers Odysseus: "Stranger, this *kēr* of mine in my chest is not such as to be angered without reason" (7.308f.); Odysseus' "*kēr* pondered in his *phrenes*" (18.344). *Ētor* is the least physical of these organs; it is located in the chest (ii.188), the *phrenes* (viii.413) and the *kardia* (xx.169).

The Soul Animals

The free soul was sometimes imagined in the shape of an animal. This puzzling phenomenon is not easy to understand. Hultkrantz gives the following explanation:

The most important of the non-human forms in which the free-soul is manifested is without doubt the theriomorphic one. The conception of the theriomorphic free-soul constitutes in a way a

---

[138] Böhme, *Die Seele und das Ich*, 63-69; T. Bolelli, "Il valore semasio-logico delle voci ἦτορ, κῆρ e κραδίη nell' epos omerico," *Annali della Scuola normale e superiore di Pisa*, 1st ser. 17 (1948) 65-75; Onians, *The Origins of European Thought*, 80-82; Chantraine, *Dictionnaire étymologique*, s.v. *ētor*; Claus, *Toward the Soul*, 22-46.

link towards the belief in the transmigration of souls. Not that the deceased person in the shape of an animal is to be understood as a continuation of the form assumed by his free-soul during his life-time. But the free-soul in animal form and the deceased person in animal form have presumably the same psychological (hallucinatory, illusionary, incidentally associative) cause. In both cases it is practically impossible to distinguish between the animal as the form in which the soul or the ghost is manifested and the animal as the dwelling of the soul or the ghost. The notions here merge insensibly into each other.[139]

Hultkrantz's explanation is not completely satisfactory. The soul's appearance in the shape of a bear or a raven is more likely to be a case of transmigration, since the body cannot contain these animals. It is more plausible to see in a soul animal of small dimensions a manifestation of the soul rather than an indication of a transmigrating soul since the soul usually leaves the body through the mouth or the nose. Furthermore, Hultkrantz's explanation does not sufficiently stress the fleeting nature of these small animals. Their transitory nature does not point to hallucinations or illusions, relatively restricted phenomena, but to dreams: the fleeting nature of the dreams reflects itself in the fleeting nature of the animals.

There is a great variety in the small soul animals. In Central Europe the mouse was by far the most dominant; farther to the east insects played a more prominent role, and in Siberia the mouse did not occur as a soul animal at all. The nature of the insects varied by country. In Japan the bee, the wasp, and the dragonfly functioned as soul animal, in Estonia the dung-beetle, and in Ireland the butterfly. Yet the evidence is still very incomplete for Europe and Asia, and virtually absent for the rest of the world.[140]

[139] Hultkrantz, *Conceptions of the soul*, 278f.
[140] H. Lixfeld, "Die Guntramsage (AT 1645A)," *Fabula* 13 (1972) 60-107.

Tentatively, we may distinguish between two categories of soul animals.[141] On the one hand there are the bee, the wasp, the fly, and similar small insects that in antiquity and later were often not sharply distinguished. In European legends these animals are not bound to the body and they represent the owner in his full identity. We may consider these as representing the free soul. On the other hand there are the animals that, originally, were supposed to exist inside the living body, like the mouse, which seems to have been considered by some peoples as the carrier of life. For example, people in some parts of Finland held that the twitching of the eye or the moving of a muscle (from the Latin *musculus*, or "little mouse") was caused by the *elohiiri*, or "life-mouse," whose presence guaranteed the continuation of life.[142] The mouse may also be compared to those animals that seem to have come into existence only at the hour of death such as the snake in Greece or the butterfly in Estonia. These animals seem to represent the body souls.

This distinction creates at least some order in a seemingly chaotic world of insects, reptiles, and small mammals. However, the distinction is largely a theoretical one, for among many peoples contaminations between the two categories have taken place. When other ideas concerning the personality and the causes of life originated, the boundaries between the two categories became blurred.

In ancient Greece we do not find the soul of a living person imagined as an insect. It has been suggested that the soul

[141] See H. Wagenvoort, *Inspiratie door bijen in de droom*, Mededelingen der Koninklijke Nederlandse Akademie van Wetenschappen, Afdeling Letterkunde, Nieuwe Reeks, vol. 29, pt. 8 (Amsterdam 1966) 22ff.

[142] Toivonen, "Spuren primitiven Seelenvorstellungen," 208; A. Vilkuna, *Das Verhalten der Finnen in "heiligen" Situationen* (Helsinki 1956) 113-115.

of Hermotimos appeared as a fly because he is discussed in Lucian's *Panegyric to the Fly* (7), but this can hardly be called a convincing argument.[143]

Conclusion

What exactly was the early Greek concept of the soul? Greek soul belief of the Archaic Age was dualistic: it still separated two elements, the free soul and the body souls that together constitute the modern concept of the soul. The word *psychē* corresponds most with Arbman's concept of the free soul, although the activity of the soul in trance and dream, which we should have expected in the light of Arbman's definition, is only evident in post-Homeric times. Considering the fragmentary state of the sources we could perhaps hardly have expected this to be otherwise.

The Greeks, then, displayed in the earliest stages of their soul belief the same broad categories that Arbman and his pupils came across in their research. However, the complexity in the Homeric epic of the free soul *psychē* and the body souls *thymos, noos,* and *menos* shows that Arbman's description of the soul as dualistic is limited, as one of Arbman's critics rightly observed.[144] Instead Greek soul belief might best be characterized as multiple. The Greeks separated where other traditions do not and a unitary soul can only be found in the period after the Archaic Age.

Finally, the early multiple nature of the soul offers a new perspective from which to view the debate about the Greek conception of the psychic whole. Bruno Snell has maintained that the early Greeks did not yet know any concept denoting the psychic whole (see Chapter One). Opponents of Snell's thesis have rightly argued that the early Greeks could easily say "I wish" or "I thought" and, consequently,

---

[143] Against H. Wagenvoort, *Inspiratie door bijen*, 24f.
[144] Fischer, *Studien über Seelenvorstellungen*, 52-54.

must have had a general sense of psychic coherence and, at least, an imperfect notion of the unity of the personality.[145] Snell also neglected the importance of the individual's name: Homer speaks of a named individual's *psychē, thymos,* and *noos.*[146] On the other hand, in Homer's time the individual did not yet know of the will as an ethical factor, nor did he distinguish between what was inside and outside himself as we do.[147] When referring to themselves, the early Greeks, like other Indo-European peoples, did not primarily consider themselves to be independent individuals but rather members of a group.[148] Yet, this argument can also be carried too far. Greek mythology presents numerous heroes who defy the norms of gods and men, such as Ajax, Achilles, and Bellerophon; these heroes are often depicted as marginal figures,[149] but their prominence shows that early Greece

[145] G. Devereux, quoted by H. Lloyd-Jones, *The Justice of Zeus* (Berkeley, London, and Los Angeles 1971) 168 n. 42; K. J. Dover, *Greek Popular Morality in the Time of Plato and Aristotle* (Oxford 1974) 151 n. 5.

[146] For the name, see M. Mauss, *Oeuvres,* vol. 2 (Paris 1969) 131-135; P. Marti, "Le nom et la personne chez les Sabé (Dahomey)," in *La notion de personne en Afrique noire* (Paris 1973) 321-326.

[147] For the will, see J. C. Opstelten, *Beschouwingen naar aanleiding van het ontbreken van ons ethisch wilsbegrip in de oud-Griekse ethiek,* Mededelingen der Koninklijke Nederlandse Akademie van Wetenschappen, Afdeling Letterkunde, Nieuwe Reeks, vol. 22, pt. 1 (Amsterdam 1959); J.-P. Vernant and P. Vidal-Naquet, *Mythe et tragédie en Grèce ancienne* (Paris 1972) 41-74; Verdenius, "Archaische denkpatronen 3," 105f.; Dover, *Greek Popular Morality,* 151 suggests that the Greeks "did not find that any useful purpose was served by attempting to distinguish an ingredient other than wishing, choosing and enthusiasm in the directional aspect of thought and action." Surely, the problem is slightly more complicated than that. For the connection between the will and the development of the self, also see A. C. Fellman and M. Fellman, "The Primacy of the Will in Late Nineteenth-Century American Ideology of the Self," *Historical Reflections* 4 (1977) 27-44. For the distinction between inside and outside, see L. Graz, "L'Iliade et la personne," *Esprit* 28 (1960) 1390-1403; Verdenius, "Archaische denkpatronen 3," 106f.

[148] E. Benveniste, *Le vocabulaire des institutions indo-européennes,* 2 vols. (Paris 1969) 1:328-333.

[149] See A. Brelich, *Gli eroi greci* (Rome 1958).

must have known numerous independent individuals. However, it is beyond the scope of this investigation to discuss problems concerning the notion of the unity of the self; still, the fact remains that the Greeks perceived the attributes of their personalities to be structured differently than we perceive ours today.[150] It is only in fifth-century Athens that we start to find the idea that the citizen can determine his own, independent course of action.[151] By the end of that century *psychē* became the center of consciousness, a development not yet fully explained but upon which, most likely, a strong influence was exerted by the rise of literacy and the growth of political consciousness.[152] And it seems likely that the systematic reflection on the soul started precisely at the end of that century because the *psychē* had become the center of consciousness and for that reason would have provoked a much stronger interest than before.[153]

[150] We are in need of a study that relates the structural elements of Archaic Greek society to the emotional realities of that society, such as has been attempted for a modern Greek village by J. Du Boulay, *Portrait of a Greek Mountain Village* (Oxford 1974) 73ff. Many perceptive observations on the historical development of the notion of personality can be found in I. Meyerson (ed.), *Problèmes de la personne* (Paris 1973); also see M. Mauss, *Sociologie et anthropologie*, 1st ed. 1938 (Paris 1959) 331-362; C. Morris, *The Discovery of the Individual 1050-1200* (London 1972); the studies quoted in note 146; C. Lévi-Strauss (ed.), *L'Identité* (Paris 1977).

[151] See Snell, *Entdeckung des Geistes*, 286.

[152] For *psychē* as center of consciousness, see the studies quoted in note 29. For the implications of literacy, see C. R. Hallpike, "Is there a primitive mentality?" *Man* 11 (1976) 253-270, and especially J. Goody, *The Domestication of the Savage Mind* (Cambridge 1977). For an up-to-date bibliography of early Greek literacy, see J. Bremmer, "Literacy and the Origins and Limitations of Greek Atheism," in J. den Boeft and A. Kessels (eds.), *Actus: Studies in Honour of H.L.W. Nelson* (Utrecht 1982) 43-55. For the political consciousness, see Vernant and Vidal-Naquet, *Mythe et tragédie*, 41-74.

[153] For this reflection, see F. Sarri, *Socrate e la genesi storica dell' idea occidentale di anima*, 2 vols. (Rome 1975) 1: 95-211, and 2: 119-186.

After the end of that century there is no longer the whole complex of the dualistic concept of the soul: a free soul representing the individuality in sleep, swoons, and trance without any contact with the ego souls, *thymos, noos,* and *menos.* This does not mean to say that in some parts of Greece elements of "primitive" soul belief could not have lingered on. In modern Europe, too, elements of primitive soul belief persist in tales of bilocation and the soul wandering off during sleep (see Appendix Two). It does mean, however, that if these elements lingered on, they existed alongside a different concept of the soul, the unitary one, a concept absent in the period before systematic reflection on the soul began.

Three

THE SOUL OF THE
DEAD

THE SOUL of the dead has not recently received the same systematic attention as the soul of the living. The great monographs on soul belief in North America and Oceania have discussed it only in short chapters,[1] and Ivar Paulson, Arbman's pupil, who intended to investigate this question systematically on a scale similar to his great study of the soul of the living in North Eurasia, died before finishing the project. However, he did publish some preliminary articles that give an indication of how he intended to proceed with his analysis of the soul of the dead.[2] By identifying the elements of the complex forming the soul and corresponding with the Western concept of the soul that survived and represented the individual after death he showed that in many instances the free soul of the living continues as the soul of the dead.[3] To give two examples, the word for the

[1] Å. Hultkrantz, *Conceptions of the soul among North American Indians* (Stockholm 1953) 464-480; H. Fischer, *Studien über Seelenvorstellungen in Ozeanien* (Munich 1965) 279-298.

[2] I. Paulson, "Seelenvorstellungen und Totenglaube," *Ethnos* 25 (1960) 85-118 and "Seelenvorstellungen und Totenglaube der permischen und wolga-finnischen Völker," *Numen* 11 (1964) 212-242.

[3] Similarly Hultkrantz, *Conceptions of the soul*, 469; Fischer, *Studien über Seelenvorstellungen*, 280. Rohde had also linked the free soul of the living and the dead but Otto denied the link and his opinion was followed

free soul among the Mordvins, a tribe in the Altai, is *ört*. Since the soul of the dead is also called *ört*, the conclusion can be drawn that the idea of the soul of the dead was derived generically from the soul of the living. Among the Japanese Ainu the original ego soul *ramat* developed into a secondary free soul, which is the soul of the dead who are also called *ramat*.

Paulson's method of investigation has its limitations. His approach is much influenced by the Western concept of the soul since he accepted as universal a common Western belief that, after death, the soul represents the individual. But there are other peoples for whom either the body survives, or the deceased are said to become theriomorphic beings, spirits, or revenants. In some places, too, the terminology for the soul of the dead is completely different from that of the living.[4] Paulson also purposely abstained from discussing the connection between the soul of the dead and the dead body. Consequently he was able to avoid discussing the actual content of man's idea about the soul of the dead. Since it is the body that is a living force in the community, it is likely that ideas about the dead body have some influence on the representation of the soul.[5]

---

by Nilsson, see W. F. Otto, *Die Manen oder von den Urformen des Totenglaubens* (Berlin 1923) 40; M. P. Nilsson, *Geschichte der griechischen Religion*, 3rd ed. vol. 1, (Munich 1967) 192.

[4] The difference is stressed by Fischer, *Studien über Seelenvorstellungen*, 297f.

[5] The transmigration of the soul is a relatively late, speculative doctrine that originally did not belong to Greek religion and will not be discussed here. On the other hand I cannot help agreeing with Burkert that the existence of this doctrine presupposes that in living beings, be they man or animal, there is an individual and permanent "something" preserving its own identity independently from the body. The body may decay, but this "something" keeps itself intact. The existence of such a "something," the *psychē*, becomes, I suggest, much more understandable against the background of my interpretation of *psychē* as the Greek version of the

Other scholars such as Nilsson have believed that soul belief can be inferred from a consideration of funeral rites.[6] Rites and customs can indeed express corresponding concepts, but the concept that once corresponded to the rite can also change or be lost. In different cultures similar rites correspond to different concepts. A rite can be performed because it is considered traditional, and there may or may not have been an earlier concept explaining it; invading peoples may have taken over rites from the earlier inhabitants without accepting the corresponding beliefs. Postulating beliefs only on the basis of the funeral rites then must be done very carefully. It seems safe to make postulates only when these rites are accompanied by contemporary explanations. These explanations do not need to be right, but they will at least indicate a current belief. Yet, however cautious we must be, the funeral rites can certainly not be left out of account, for already in 1907 Robert Hertz demonstrated that among the peoples of Indonesia and many others funeral rites were thought to aid the transition of the soul from the world of the living to the world of the world of the dead.[7]

concept of the free soul than if *psychē* was purely the breath or the life principle. See W. Burkert, *Griechische Religion der archaischen und klassischen Epoche* (Stuttgart 1977) 446; also see C. Hopf, *Antike Seelenwanderungsvorstellungen* (Diss. Univ. of Leipzig 1934); W. Stettner, *Die Seelenwanderung bei Griechen und Römern* (Stuttgart and Berlin 1934); H. S. Long, "A Study of the Doctrine of Metempsychosis in Greece from Pythagoras to Plato" (Diss. Princeton Univ. 1948); W. Burkert, *Lore and Science in Ancient Pythagoreanism* (Cambridge, Mass. 1972) 120-136 and *Griechische Religion*, 443-447; J. Barnes, *The presocratic philosophers*, vol. 1 (London 1979) 100-120.

[6] Nilsson, *Geschichte*, 174; compare also A. Schnaufer, *Frühgriechischer Totenglaube* (Hildesheim and New York 1970) 34-57.

[7] R. Hertz, *Death and the Right Hand* (London 1960) 27-86, 117-154. Hertz was one of the many members of the circle around Durkheim who did not survive the First World War, see E. Durkheim, "Notice sur Robert Hertz," *L'Annuaire des anciens élèves de l'Ecole Normale Supérieure* 1916,

Taking these preliminary considerations into account, in this chapter we shall develop in detail the following outline of the early Greek views of the soul of the dead. Of all the elements of the soul described earlier for the soul of the living, it is the free soul in the form of *psychē* that becomes identified as the soul of the dead. The soul of the dead was not dual or multiple and lacked the psychological traits associated with *thymos, noos,* and *menos.* And the development toward a unitary soul for the soul of the living does not correspond with a change in the concept of the soul of the dead. The *psychē* leaves the body at the moment of death and begins an afterlife. After death, however, the deceased is presented not only as *psychē* but also as an *eidōlon* or compared to shadows. Occasionally the body itself represents the deceased in an afterlife and there are reports associating the dead with the snake.

It is the physical attributes of the soul that have some importance for the Greeks rather than the psychological. The descriptions of the *eidōlon* suggests that the Greeks believed the dead soul looked like the living being. And they described the physical actions of the souls of the dead in two opposite ways: they believed both that the dead souls moved and spoke like the living and that the soul of the dead could not move or speak but instead flitted and squeaked.

The funeral rites of the Greeks functioned as a rite of passage for the soul from the world of the living to the afterlife. Souls of those who died without being full members of the social order such as criminals, children, and adolescents were not given full funeral rites and were not thought to enter fully into the world of the dead. Yet, as we shall see, there is little evidence that those who died outside

116-120; E. E. Evans-Pritchard in Hertz, ibidem, 9-24 and *A History of Anthropological Thought* (New York 1981) 170-183.

the ordered social world remained to haunt the living as ghosts or revenants.

The Soul at the Moment of Death

Of all the elements of the soul only the *psychē* continues in an afterlife and represents the individual. And of all these elements it is precisely the *psychē* which, as shown above, corresponds most closely to Arbman's definition of the free soul. This suggests that for the Greeks as for many other peoples the free soul of the living was the same as the soul of the dead. The souls of the dead, however, lacked the psychological elements associated with the ego souls of the soul of the living.

In Homer when someone dies, the *psychē* leaves and does not return. After Hyperenor had been fatally hit, his *psychē* quickly left him (xIV.518). In the cases of Patroclus (xVI.856), Hector (xXII.362), and Elpenor (10.560 and 11.65) Homer adds that the *psychē* went to Hades. In these cases the *psychē* always leaves the body under its own power. Only in the case of Andromache's swoon is it said that she blew forth her *psychē* (xXII.467). When Pandaros was killed by Diomedes, his *psychē* and *menos* were "loosened" (v.296). It seems that here the act of being "loosened," which is more appropriate to *menos* (see below), has been transferred to *psychē*.

In the actual epic descriptions of the moment of death the *aiōn* is never mentioned, yet death must have been closely connected with the absence of the *aiōn* because death is expressed as the departure of the *aiōn* (v.685; 7.224) or the deprivation of the *aiōn* (xXII.58). Achilles is afraid that the maggots will defile the dead body of Patroclus "for the *aiōn* has been slain out" (xIX.27).

At the moment of death the individual also loses his *thymos*. This process can be expressed in different ways. After

Dioreus had been fatally hit "he fell backwards in the dust
. . . while he blew forth his *thymos*" (XIII.654). Sometimes
the *thymos* departs under its own power. Ajax hit Sarpedon's comrade-in-arms Epikles, who "like an acrobat fell
down from the high wall, and the *thymos* left his bones"
(XII.386). Sometimes it is said that the *thymos* is taken out
of or away from the body. Diomedes slew the sons of Phae-
nops and "took out the *thymos* from both" (V.155). Later
on he killed Axylos and his servant and "from both he took
away the *thymos*" (VI.17).

What happens to the *thymos* once it has left the body
remains completely obscure. Unlike *psychē* it never goes to
Hades, with which it is connected only once. Nestor lets
Peleus wish "that his *thymos* might go from his limbs into
the house of Hades" (VII.131). This expression, though,
seems to be a rhetorical wish and not a reflection of normal
belief.[8] Finally, it is not without importance to observe that
when someone is killed, or the wish to kill is expressed, it
is more often the *thymos* than the *psychē* which is mentioned as having left the body. This supports our earlier
analysis of the role and place of the *psychē* of the living:
when an individual is normally active the *psychē* is hardly
thought of.[9]

Although today there exists great interest in the presence
or absence of the mind at the moment of dying, the *noos*
is never mentioned in Homeric descriptions of death. The
poet always characterizes death by describing the departure
of the *psychē, thymos,* or *menos.* Since the *noos* was con-

---

[8] R. B. Onians, *The Origins of European Thought,* 2nd ed. (Cambridge
1954) 93; W. J. Verdenius, "Archaische denkpatronen 3," *Lampas* 5 (1972)
116 n. 23. B. Snell, *Die Entdeckung des Geistes,* 4th ed. (Göttingen 1974)
21 considers it a case of later poetic contamination.

[9] This becomes very apparent from the ratio of *thymos* and *psychē* in
the Homeric epic which is 9.3:1 (the counting is based on the Concord-
ances of Prendergast and Dunbar). This ratio is even rather distorted in
favor of *psychē* by the high occurrence of *psychē* in *Odyssey* 11 and 24.

nected more vaguely with the body than the other "souls," such as the *thymos* and *menos*, this is hardly surprising.

Death naturally puts an end to the activity of the *menos*, but unlike *psychē* and *thymos*, *menos* is never said to leave the body. Its activity is invariably said to be "loosened, unharnessed," a metaphor comparing the collapsing of the dead with the collapsing of horses when they are unharnessed after a tiring ride (the verb used, *lyō*, is especially used for the unharnessing and unyoking of horses, oxen etc.). After Pandaros had fallen from his chariot, his horses became frightened by his shining armor and "from him straightway his *psychē* and *menos* were loosened" (v.296). Homer uses the same expression to describe the end of Eniopeus (VIII.123) and Archeptolemos (VIII.315).

The ego potencies are of less interest. Excluding the references where a clear physical meaning is indicated, only *ētor* is mentioned, the least physical of the ego potencies. Achilles left Xanthus lying in the sand "since he had taken away his *ētor*" (XXI.201). The same expression is used for the dead Hector (XXIV.50) when Achilles drags him round Patroclus' grave.

It is not surprising that after death nothing is said of the body souls. Their connection with the body is the cause of their disappearance. Outside Greece it sometimes does happen, though, that a body soul survives after death. In the case of those peoples with a thoroughly dualistic soul belief the body soul never represents the person's real personality but turns, for example, into a spook.

Human and Theriomorphic Manifestations of the Deceased

As we have seen, *psychē* represented the identity of the deceased; the dead in the afterlife are indeed often called *psychai* (11.84, 90 etc.).[10] However, *psychē* is not the only term in use for the dead, nor is the moment of death expressed only in terms of a *psychē* leaving the body. In Homer the body sometimes represents the individual; the dead are compared to shadows, and the term *eidōlon* is used to describe the soul of the deceased. There is some evidence, too, to indicate that the Greeks believed the soul of the dead to be embodied in the snake.

After Agamemnon had killed the sons of Antenor, Iphidamas and Koön, "they went into the house of Hades" (XI.263). Here, then, it is not *psychē* but the persons themselves who are said to have gone to Hades. A similar idea may be behind those expressions where the dead are referred to as "*menos*-less heads of the dead" (10.521; 11.29, 49), for the head sometimes functioned as *pars pro toto*.

Although the idea is rare in Homer, the phenomenon is not uncommon elsewhere. Hultkrantz has written: "Various pronouncements by Indians from different parts of America testify to the fact that the souls' identification with the deceased has not been self-evident and immediately given: we are told that the person survives, and if there are the beginnings of an indication of the roles played by the souls in the transition to the new existence opinion is not infrequently divided, confused and contradictory."[11] In some areas of Oceania, too, it was not the free soul but the *homo totus* that became the soul of the dead.[12] Given the paucity of material on the period it is impossible to draw a firm conclusion, but it seems that in Homeric times, too, traces of such a belief were still visible.[13]

---

[10] It is therefore very striking that in a papyrus fragment (P. *Köln* 3.125), which probably derives from Aeschylus' *Psychagogoi*, the *psychai* of the dead are called *apsychoi*, or "life-less," see H. Lloyd-Jones, ZPE 42 (1981) 21; J. S. Rusten, ZPE 45 (1982) 36 n. 10.

[11] Hultkrantz, *Conceptions of the soul*, 465.

[12] Fischer, *Studien über Seelenvorstellungen*, 280.

[13] Similarly Otto, *Die Manen*, 33.

Among a number of peoples the dead are called "shadows." However, Homer only compares the dead to a shadow. After Circe had told Odysseus that Teiresias was the only one in Hades with a *noos*, she added: "but the others (i.e. the other people in Hades) flit like shadows (10.495).[14] And when Odysseus wanted to embrace his mother in the Underworld, she flew away "like a shadow or a dream" (11.207f.).

The relationship between the soul of the dead and the shadow is still in need of a systematic discussion based upon large-scale exploitation of the anthropological material.[15] Hultkrantz observes that in some quarters it is stressed that the physical shadow becomes a ghost after death, but as a rule there is no such identity. In most cases in which the dead person is represented as a shadow there is no continuity between the shadow of the living individual and the "shade" of the deceased, and so the term "shadow" is only a metaphor. These observations of Hultkrantz are fully supported by the (admittedly scarce) Homeric material.[16]

Sometimes the word *eidōlon* is used.[17] Patroclus com-

---

[14] Onians, *The Origins of European Thought*, 95 and G. van der Leeuw, *Phänomenologie der Religion*, 2nd ed. (Tübingen 1956) 325 identify the dead with the shadow, but in that case it would be suggested that Teiresias was *not* a *skia*, or "shadow."

[15] For the shadow, see E. L. Rochholz, *Deutscher Glaube und Brauch im Spiegel der heidnischen Vorzeit*, vol. 1 (Berlin 1867) 59-130; J. von Negelein, "Bild, Spiegel und Schatten im Volksglauben," *Archiv für Religionswissenschaft* 5 (1902) 1-37; F. Pradel, "Der Schatten im Volksglauben," *Mitteilungen der schlesischen Gesellschaft für Volkskunde* 6, no. 12 (1904) 1-41; J. G. Frazer, *Taboo and the Perils of the Soul*, 3rd ed. (London 1911) 77-100; L. Bieler, "Schatten," in H. Bächtold-Stäubli (ed.), *Handwörterbuch der deutschen Aberglaube*, vol. 9 (Berlin 1938-1941) 126-142; B. George, *Zu den altägyptischen Vorstellungen vom Schatten als Seele* (Bonn 1970); P. W. van der Horst, "Der Schatten im hellenistischen Volksglauben," in M. J. Vermaseren (ed.), *Studies in Hellenistic Religions* (Leiden 1979) 27-36.

[16] Hultkrantz, *Conceptions of the soul*, 305.

[17] Otto, *Die Manen*, 34; Nilsson, *Geschichte*, 195.

plained to Achilles that the "*eidōla* of those who have been worn out" prevented him from entering the gates of Hades (XXIII.72, 11.476, 24.14). During his visit to Hades Odysseus spoke with the *eidōlon* of his friend Elpenor (11.83). And after the bloody end of the suitors, the seer Theoclymenos saw the doorway to the court filled with *eidōla* (20.355).

The meaning of *eidōlon* becomes clear from two passages. After Apollo had taken Aeneas away to a temple to be healed after a fight against Diomedes, "he made an *eidōlon* like Aeneas himself" (v.450). Athena sent Penelope an *eidōlon* which she made like Iphthime (4.796). From these passages it appears that an *eidōlon* is a being that looks exactly like a person. This becomes especially clear in the case of Achilles when he is visited by the *psychē* of Patroclus in a dream. When Patroclus departs, Achilles tries to embrace him, but Patroclus' *psychē* vanishes without Achilles succeeding. He then realizes that it was a "*psychē* and *eidōlon*," although "it was wondrous like him" (XXIII.104-107). The word *eidōlon*, thus, originally stressed the fact that for the ancient Greeks the dead looked exactly like the living. Democritus, however, could already use the word for ghosts with a supernatural appearance.[18]

In Homer the term *eidōlon* is never used for the souls of the living.[19] It is found only for the living in the fragment of Pindar cited in Chapter One. In the dirge to which this fragment belongs Pindar is naturally concerned with the fate of the dead.[20] It is therefore not surprising that he uses

[18] Democritus B 166 Diels/Kranz; see P. J. Bicknell, "Democritus' Theory of Precognition," *Revue des études grecques* 82 (1969) 318-326; W. Burkert, *Illinois Classical Studies* 2 (1977) 108.

[19] Against E. Bickel, *Homerischer Seelenglaube* (Berlin 1925) 315f.; O. Regenbogen, *Kleine Schriften* (Munich 1961) 17.

[20] For the fragment, see F. Graf, *Eleusis und die orphische Dichtung Athens in vorhellenistischer Zeit*, RGVV, vol. 33 (Berlin and New York)

eidōlon for the soul in general, first for that part of the individual that survives death "for this alone has come from the gods," then for the same part already manifesting itself during lifetime. The divine origin of the *eidōlon* will have been Pindar's explanation for the continuity of the soul of the living—if he did not derive the idea from the doctrines of the transmigration of the soul.[21]

The deceased was occasionally thought to assume the form of an animal, and in the first decades of this century there existed a lively interest in these theriomorphic manifestations that led to the identification (more often than not untenable) of all kinds of animals with the soul of the dead. It is the great merit of Nilsson to have radically rejected all these identifications, since for virtually none of them was there convincing evidence that a soul of the dead was really meant. The only animal retained by Nilsson, and that unequivocally can be considered to have been a soul animal in Archaic Greece, is the snake. As a soul animal it was especially connected with the grave and above all with the grave of the hero.[22] This particular function of the snake developed from its position as protector of the house, although the Greeks themselves sometimes suggested that the marrow of a dead body changed into a snake.[23] The snake probably already functioned as the protector of the house in Neolithic times. It was still regarded in this way

---

86 n. 31; for dirges in general, see G. Nagy, *The Best of the Achaeans* (Baltimore and London 1979) 170-172.

[21] Burkert, *Griechische Religion*, 446.

[22] Nilsson, *Geschichte*, 197-199; also see E. Küster, *Die Schlange in der griechischen Kunst und Religion*, RGVV, vol. 13, no. 2 (Giessen 1913). For the later grave reliefs in which the snake and the deceased are often pictured together, see Nilsson, ibidem, 199); E. Mitropolou, *Horses' Heads and Snakes in Banquet Reliefs and their Meaning* (Athens 1976) 83-145 and *Deities and Heroes in the Form of Snakes* (Athens 1977).

[23] Nilsson, *Geschichte*, 198. On marrow, see Ovid *Metamorphoses* 15.389; Pliny *Natural History* 10.56.86; Plutarch *Cleomenes* 39; Aelian *De natura animalium* 1.51; Origen *Contra Celsum* 4.57; Servius *Aeneis* 5.95.

in large parts of northern and southern Europe in the early part of this century.[24]

The classical discussions of the snake as the soul of the dead are not quite satisfactory for this investigation, since they use the term "soul" without reflecting on the relationship between the *psychē* as the soul of the dead and the snake. If the deceased was normally thought to be represented by the *psychē* in the underworld, what then was the position of the snake? Was a person perhaps at one time thought to have a double existence after death?

The only possible example of such an existence is Heracles, whose *eidōlon* was seen by Odysseus in the underworld but who himself was living among the immortal gods (11.602-604). However, this passage looks like a late construction, set up in order to explain different traditions about Heracles, and can hardly be considered as an expression of original soul belief since, as Hultkrantz observes,

The deceased in the realm of the dead is always considered to continue the existence and consciousness of the dead person. . . . The same person can thus, in genuine belief, not at the same time figure in two realms of the dead (I am here of course thinking of the belief held by one and the same individual). In naïve belief the ghost remaining at the grave or other places in the vicinity of the living may be taken as the adequate form of expression for the deceased himself, especially as the dead person is sometimes conceived as returning to the living. If, however, the connection between soul and spook-ghost be emphasized, the latter appears as a distorted by-product, a remote echo of the departed individual,

[24] J. Maringer, "Die Schlange in Kunst und Kult der vorgeschichtlichen Menschen," *Anthropos* 72 (1977) 881-920; M. P. Nilsson, *Greek Folk Religion*, 1st ed., 1940 (New York 1961) 67-72; L. Honko, "Ormkult," in *Kulturhistorisk leksikon for Nordisk Middelalder*, vol. 13 (Copenhagen 1968) 8-10; V. Rusu, "Un chapitre de la mythologie Roumaine: 'le serpent de maison,' " *Revue des langues romanes* 82 (1977) 257-267. It is curious to note that although milk was often offered to house snakes, snakes do not seem to like milk, see W. La Barre, *They shall take up serpents*, 1st ed., 1962 (New York 1969) 94f.

not as his real ego, his personality. About the same applies to the other forms of the deceased as to the spook-ghost: according to the degree of reflection and to the occurrence of definite associations to one of the souls of the living individual they are understood as being more or less identical with him.[25]

Unfortunately our sources are not very informative about the cult of the dead and we simply do not know what or even if the Greeks of the Archaic Age thought about the precise connection of the snake with the soul and body of the dead, although in naïve belief the snake was evidently taken as the deceased himself.

Aristotle (*Historia Animalium* 551 A) indicates that the word *psychē* also meant "butterfly." Curiously, this seems to be the only word for butterfly known by the Greeks—a fact that has been insufficiently taken into account by Nilsson;[26] consequently, the meaning will be older than its first occurrence suggests. Unfortunately, there are no other indications of a possible connection between the butterfly and the soul of the living and the dead. It seems that in Minoan times—but the evidence is debated—the butterfly stood in some relationship to the dead, but this of course does not prove that the butterfly was indeed conceived of as a soul of the dead in the period under investigation.[27] The possibility should not be excluded, however.

The Relation Between the Soul and the Body of the Dead

Hultkrantz observes, "At death, the person emerges in a new form of existence, no soul-idea is needed to mediate

[25] Hultkrantz, *Conceptions of the soul,* 473.

[26] Nilsson, *Geschichte,* 198.

[27] B. C. Dietrich, *The Origins of Greek Religion* (Berlin and New York 1974) 119-122; J. Gwynn Griffiths, *The Divine Tribunal* (Swansea 1975) 15f.

this transition, for it is the person himself who goes on living in the new existence."[28] Hultkrantz is only partially right, at least regarding the Greek material. It is certainly true that there is a corollary of this idea in the *Nekuia* where Heracles (11.601-627) and Orion (11.572-575) are depicted as continuing their earthly activities, but there are also other representations that are not so easy to understand if we follow Hultkrantz. The dead, for example, in Homer cannot speak in a normal manner, neither do they move in the normal way. How can these features be reconciled with Hultkrantz's definition of the deceased as a memory image of an earlier existing person? Here, Hultkrantz's analysis is somewhat deficient, in so far as he has failed to identify the factors constituting the memory image of the deceased and to take into account the difference between the memories of a living person and a dead one. Memories of the dead are not only influenced by, for example, the way they spoke, moved, or laughed when still alive but also by the way they were at the moment of death when they did not speak, move, or laugh. In fact, both memories seem to have created the memory image of the deceased for the early Greeks.

The great importance of the moment of death is very much apparent in the description of the appearance of the dead with wounds exactly as they received them just before they died. Homer describes the warriors at the entrance to Hades still dressed in their bloody armor (11.41). Similar descriptions can also be found after Homeric times; Aeschylus has the *eidōlon* of Clytemnestra display her death wounds (*Eumenides* 103), and Plato elaborately explains this idea, but refines it in a way by adding that the soul also retains the scars of its former existence.[29] The same theme

---

[28] Hultkrantz, *Conceptions of the soul*, 464.

[29] Plato *Gorgias* 524-25, see E. R. Dodds, *Plato, Gorgias* (Oxford 1959) 379.

is found on vases, where the dead are regularly shown with their wounds, sometimes still bandaged.[30] Among the Romans descriptions of the souls of the dead with their wounds became a very popular topos.[31]

The great importance of the *sōma*, or "dead body," for the representation of the soul of the dead is also apparent in other descriptions.[32] The souls of the dead lacked the psychological attributes of the souls of the living. Since the *thymos* left the individual at the moment of death it is understandable that we never hear of any soul of the dead with a *thymos*. Neither do the dead possess a *noos* (10.494-495) or a *menos*—the dead are called "*menos*-less heads" (10.493-495, 521, 536).[33] The only exception is Teiresias (10.493-496). As a seer he fell outside the normal community of the living, as has recently been convincingly argued; for that reason he also stands outside the community of the dead.[34]

Not only do the souls of the dead lack the "souls" and organs connected with an inner life, but other faculties and qualities are also absent. They are unable to speak prop-

[30] J. Chamay, "Des défunts portant bandages," *Bulletin Antieke Beschaving* 52-53 (1977-78) 247-251.

[31] Virgil *Aeneid* 2.270-79, 6.446, 450, and 494; Tibullus 1.10.37, 2.6.38-40; Propertius 4.7.7; Ovid *Metamorphoses* 10.49; Statius *Silvae* 2.1.154-56; Silius Italicus 12.547-550; Apuleius *Metamorphoses* 8.8.

[32] It is debated whether *sōma* can also mean "living body," see H. Herter, *Kleine Schriften* (Munich 1975) 91-105; S. R. Slings, *ZPE* 18 (1975) 170; M. L. West, *Hesiod, Works and Days* (Oxford 1978) 295; R. Renehan, "The Meaning of σῶμα in Homer: a Study in Methodology," *California Studies in Classical Antiquity* 12 (1980) 269-281.

[33] The expression was already considered obscure in Aristophanes' time: Aristophanes fragment 222 Edmonds. In A. Bernand, *Inscriptions métriques de l'Egypte gréco-romaine* (Paris 1969) no. 18.8 a dead man is called *dusmenēs*, a qualification that must be understood against this background, see A. Wilhelm, *Wiener Studien* 56 (1938) 58f.

[34] C. G. Gual, "Tiresias o el advino como mediador," *Emerita* 43 (1975) 107-132; L. Brisson, *Le mythe de Tirésias* (Leiden 1976).

erly.[35] When the soul of Patroclus left Achilles, he disappeared squeaking (XXIII.101). The same sound was made by the souls of the suitors when they were guided by Hermes to the underworld and for that reason they were compared with bats (24.5, 9). Pythagoras was supposed to have seen Hesiod "bound fast to a bronze pillar and squeaking" (Diogenes Laertius 8.21). A different sound is attributed to them by Sophocles who writes, "Up comes the swarm of the dead humming."[36] This miserable sound of the souls of the dead is obviously caused by their inability to speak. Death is indeed called "voice-robbing" by Hesiod (*Shield* 131), and Theognis (569) says that he will be as a "voiceless stone" when he lies under the earth. This theme of the silent dead is repeatedly met in later poetry, and the Romans, too, called their souls of the dead "keeping silence" or "mute."[37]

The dead move in a different way. While the individual at the moment of death no longer moves, and alive moves normally, the souls of the dead are described as "flitting" (10.495): they have a surplus of movement. Here, the living being occupies a mediating position between the dead body and the soul of the dead.

Finally, we may wonder if in the Archaic Age souls of the dead were supposed to be able to laugh. It is a widespread belief that the dead do not laugh, and that visitors to the underworld and those who have encountered shades can

[35] For the language of the souls of the dead, see H. Wagenvoort, *Inspiratie door bijen in de droom*, Mededelingen der Koninklijke Nederlandse Akademie van Wetenschappen, Afdeling Letterkunde, Nieuwe Reeks, vol. 29, pt. 8 (Amsterdam 1966) 86-88.

[36] Sophocles fragment 879 Radt.

[37] Virgil *Aeneid* 6.265; Ovid *Fasti* 2.609, 5.422; C. Bologna, "Il linguaggio del silenzio," *Studi Storico-Religiosi* 2 (1978) 305-342.

no longer laugh.[38] Laughter is still a highly underresearched subject from an anthropological and historical point of view, but recently scholars have noted the significance of laughter for constituting a group identity, and its relevance for the establishment of the level of bodily control in a particular group or culture.[39] The latter point is not without interest for the ancient world, since the fact that ascetics such as Pythagoras (Diogenes Laertius 8.20) and Christian monks did not laugh at all, or only sporadically, fits in well with the observation of the British anthropologist Mary Douglas that narrow groups with a high threshold for bodily control have difficulty in allowing themselves to laugh and so relax their control over the body.[40]

Folklorists, on the other hand, long ago noted that among many peoples laughter is a sign of life; its absence belongs

[38] W. Mannhardt, *Mythologische Forschungen* (Strassburg 1884) 99f.; Karle, in Bächtold-Stäubli (ed.), *Handwörterbuch der deutschen Aberglaube*, vol. 5 (1932-33) 874; K. Ranke, *Indogermanische Totenverehrung* (Helsinki 1951) 284f.; W. Puchner, *Brauchtumserscheinungen im griechischen Jahreslauf* (Vienna 1977) 71.

[39] G. Blaicher, "Über das Lachen im englischen Mittelalter," *Deutsche Vierteljahrsschrift für Literaturwissenschaft und Geistesgeschichte* 44 (1970) 508-529; D. S. Lichačevs, in S. S. Konkin (ed.), *Problemy poetiki i istorii literatury. Festschrift M. Bakhtin* (Saransk 1973) 73-90 (on laughter among the ancient Russians); G. McCall, *Current Anthropology* 16 (1975) 347; K. Thomas, "The Place of Laughter in Tudor and Stuart England," *Times Literary Supplement*, 21 January 1977; H. S. Versnel, "Destruction, *Devotio* and Despair in a Situation of Anomy: the Mourning for Germanicus in Triple Perspective," in G. Piccaluga (ed.), *Perennitas. Studi in onore di Angelo Brelich* (Rome 1980) 541-618, esp. 599f. suggests a connection of laughter with jokes and joking relationships, but this suggestion is not supported by the literature he quotes, and in fact it is explicitly rejected by recent students of those subjects, see M. Douglas, *Implicit Meanings* (London and Boston 1975) 92f.; R. Johnson, "Jokes, Theories, Anthropology," *Semiotica* 22 (1978) 309-334, esp. 310.

[40] *Vita Pachomii* 1st ed., 104, 121; *Vita Melaniae* 23; B. Steidle, "Das Lachen im alten Mönchtum," *Benediktinische Monatsschrift* 20 (1938) 271-280; Douglas, *Implicit Meanings*, 85.

to times and places where normal life is not present.[41] This observation is especially important for the interpretation of ritual laughter. For example, during the Roman Lupercalia the foreheads of two young men were touched with a blood-stained knife—most likely a case of symbolical killing—and they were then cleaned with wool that had been steeped in milk; finally they had to laugh. The succession from "death" to laughter strongly suggests that in this case laughter was indeed a sign of life and, possibly, even implied the incorporation into the community, since the Lupercalia seems to have developed from an ancient puberty ritual.[42] Another case of ritual laughter took place in Western Europe, where Easter Sunday used to be the occasion for all kinds of laughter and merriment, the *risus paschalis*. The laughter can hardly be separated from Jesus' return from the dead, but it will also have had a liberating effect after the serious days of Lent.[43]

In Greece evidence regarding the absence of laughter can

[41] V. J. Propp, *Edipo alla luce del folclore*, 1st ed., 1939 (Turin 1975) 41-81; also see S. Reinach, *Cultes, mythes et religions*, vol. 4 (Paris 1912) 109-129; E. Fehrle, "Das Lachen im Glauben der Völker," *Zeitschrift für Volkskunde*, n.s. 2 (1930) 1-5; N. J. Richardson, *The Homeric Hymn to Demeter* (Oxford 1974) 217; A. M. di Nola, *Antropologia religiosa* (Florence 1974) 15-90 ("Riso ed oscenità").

[42] Plutarch *Romulus* 21. For the initiatory interpretation of the Lupercalia, a highly debated festival, see A. Alföldi, *Die Struktur des voretruskischen Römerstaates* (Heidelberg 1974) 86-106; J.-P. Neraudeau, *La jeunesse dans la littérature et les institutions de la Rome républicaine* (Paris 1979) 200-215. The laughter was already interpreted as a renewal of life by Mannhardt, *Mythologische Forschungen*, 99f.; L. Deubner, *Archiv für Religionswissenschaft* 13 (1910) 501.

[43] The oldest discussion of Easter Laughter is by the Basel reformer Oecolampadius, see his *De risu paschali, Oecolampadii, ad V. Capitonem theologum epistola apologetica* (Basel 1518); the not very helpful J. P. Schmidt, *De risu paschali* (Rostock 1747); H. Fluck, "Der risus paschalis," *Archiv für Religionswissenschaft* 31 (1934) 188-212; V. Wendland, *Ostermärchen und Ostergelächter* (Bern and Frankfurt 1980).

only be found in the period after the Archaic Age. It was reported that those who had consulted the oracle of Trophonios in Lebadeia had completely lost the power to laugh during their visit. The loss was explained, at least according to Pausanias (9.39.13), by the impressive experience of the visitor, but the oracle was connected with an entrance to the Underworld; its visitors were carried out of the hole of the oracle feet first, as were corpses.[44] Since it seems unlikely that the idea of the loss of laughter was newly developed or derived from other cultures, it seems a plausible hypothesis that this notion also occurred in the Archaic Age.

The ideas, then, concerning the soul of the dead were strongly influenced by memories of the dead body. However, not all these negative qualities, such as the absence of the *noos* or a proper voice, were thought to be inherent in the souls of the dead always at one and the same time. In real life it must have been impossible to remember the dead, with whom one had been acquainted, only in this way. In these cases there must have always been memories of activities of the deceased during life that would also determine the memory image. For that reason Patroclus, who has only just died, can be described as appearing to Achilles exactly as he was during his life. And as long as he has contact with Achilles he speaks like a normal mortal; only when the contact is over does he leave squeaking.

With the passing of time the precise memories of a specific deceased person fade away, and it is understandable that the more personal traits gradually withdraw behind a

---

[44] W. H. Roscher (ed.), *Ausführliches Lexikon der griechischen und römischen Mythologie*, vol. 5 (Leipzig 1916-24) 1272; also see E. Samter, *Volkskunde im altsprachlichen Unterricht* (Berlin 1923) 120-124; U. E. Paoli, *Die Geschichte der Neaira* (Bern 1953) 39-48; Burkert, *Lore and Science*, 154 speaks of a "journey into the underworld."

more general idea of the dead as the opposite of the living.[45] In literature, be it oral or written, there is rarely a personal tie between the dead and the living, and so the negative qualities are stressed. But, here, too this is not kept up consistently, and Achilles (11.467-540) and Ajax (11.543-567) behave as if they were still alive.

Funeral Rites and The Soul

Although the inference of soul belief from funeral rites must be made carefully, there are some clear indications of the Archaic Greek ideas on the function of the funeral rites. The evidence from Homer and other sources suggests that a proper funeral functions as a rite of passage for the dead into an afterlife. In the Archaic period a funeral was not simply the burial or cremation of the body; there were a series of rites that were thought to aid the dead soul in its passage from the world of the living to the world of the dead. In addition the sources for the period indicate that some of the souls of the dead, including those of children, adolescents, and criminals, were thought to have a special status. Some of them in fact were thought to remain outside the world of the dead and not to participate fully in the transition.

When the dead Patroclus appears in a dream to Achilles, he asks to be cremated, because he may not cross the river to Hades in his unburied state (XXIII.72-76). In the *Odyssey* only Elpenor, who is still unburied, does not need to drink blood to be able to speak. Obviously he is dead but has not

[45] For the idea of the dead as the opposite of the living, also see J.-P. Vernant, *Mythe et pensée chez les Grecs*, 1st ed., 1965, 6th ed., 2 vols. (Paris 1981) 2:65-78.

yet become a full shade (11.51-83). And the same belief clearly underlies the story of Sisyphus, who instructed his wife not to perform the proper funeral rites after death so he could persuade Persephone to let him return to the land of the living.[46]

The connection between the lack of burial and the refusal of admittance to Hades is also a contributing factor to the often expressed fear of death at sea, the throwing of bodies of criminals and enemies of the state into the sea, and the denial of burial as punishment for serious crimes.[47] The most famous example of this latter punishment is of course Polyneices in Sophocles' *Antigone*, but Polyneices evidently was not the only such case since Bion says that anguish over burial was the subject of many tragedies.[48]

In Attica traitors and those guilty of sacrilege might expect to be thrown unburied over the border. This was the fate of Antiphon, the *strategoi* who did not pick up those who drowned after the battle at the Arginusae in 406, and Phocion and his friends.[49] A refusal of burial for those who

[46] Alcaeus fragment 38 Voigt; Theognis 711ff.; Pherecydes *FGrH* 3 F 119; Eustathius 1701-1702.

[47] For death at sea, see 5.308-321; Hesiod *Works and Days* 687; Archilochus fragments 9-13 West; Andocides *On the Mysteries* 137f.; Achilles Tatius 5.16; R. Lattimore, *Themes in Greek and Latin Epitaphs*, 2nd ed. (Urbana 1962) 199-201. For throwing into the sea, see G. Glotz, "Katapontismos," in C. Daremberg and E. Saglio (eds.), *Dictionnaire des antiquités grecques et romaines*, vol. 3, pt. 1 (Paris n.d.) 808-810. For the denial of burial, see Thucydides 1.136.6; Dio Chrysostomus 31.85.

[48] Bion F 70 Kindstrand. See also Sophocles *Antigone* 26-30 (Euripides *Phoenissae* 1630 mentions even a throwing over the border); Sophocles *Ajax* 1047ff.; Euripides *Suppliants*; see most recently G. Cerri, *Legislazione orale e tragedia greca* (Naples 1979).

[49] On Antiphon, see Plutarch *Moralia* 833 A; Marcellinus *Vita Thucydidis* 22. On the *strategoi*, see Teles p. 29 Hense. On Phocion, see Plutarch *Phocion* 37.3; Diodorus Siculus 18.67.6; Nepos *Phocion* 4; Valerius Maximus 5.3 ext. 3; Dio Chrysostomus 73.7.

were condemned to death was extended to the whole area of the second sea league.[50] The evidently frightening prospect of refusal of burial in Attica was even one of the arguments used in court to move the jury.[51] And the denial of burial was urged by Plato in his *Laws* (855 A) for sacrilege, homicide of a family member in the first degree after the killer had been stoned on a three-forked road (873 C), and also for other serious crimes (909 C).[52] It could even happen that the bodies of criminals were dug up and thrown out over the border as happened with the Alcmeonidae, Phrynichus (Lycurgus *Leochares* 113), and the ancestors of the Corinthian Psammetichus.[53] The practice of refusing burial also existed outside Athens; it was the fate of the mythical Boeotian king Pyraechmis at the hands of Heracles (Plutarchus *Moralia* 307 C), the Arcadian Aristocrates (Pausanias 4.22.7), Psammetichus, the Macedonian Alcetas (Diodorus Siculus 18.47.3), Hyperides, Pausanias, according to some traditions, and of sacrilegious people all over Greece, according to the Locrians (Diodorus Siculus 16.25.2).[54]

[50] W. Dittenberger, *Sylloge inscriptionum Graecarum*, 3rd ed., vol. 1 (Leipzig 1915) no. 147.

[51] Hyperides *Pro Euxenippo* 18 and *Pro Lycophrone* 20 (note also Aeschines 3.252).

[52] For the special character of a three-forked road, see Klein, in Bächtold-Stäubli (ed.), *Handwörterbuch der deutschen Aberglaube*, vol. 5 (1932-33) 516-529; M. Puhvel, "The Mystery of the Cross-Roads," *Folklore* 87 (1976) 167-177.

[53] On the Alcmeonidae, see Thucydides 1.126; Isocrates 16.26; Aristotle *Athenaion Politeia* 1; Plutarch *Solon* 12 and *Moralia* 549 A. For the ancestors of Psammetichus, see Nicolaus Damascenus *FGrH* 90 F 60.

[54] For Psammetichus, see Nicolaus Damascenus *FGrH* 90 F 60. For Hyperides, see Plutarch *Moralia* 849 C (Suidas s.v. *hyperōrion* mentions a refusal of burial in Attica). For Pausanias, see Plutarch *Moralia* 308; Aelian *Varia Historia* 4.7; J. Stobaeus, *Anthologium*, ed. O. Hense, vol. 3 (Berlin 1894) 728.

Here too the problem arises as to the connection between the mode of behavior and the motivation behind it. Undoubtedly fear of pollution was a powerful factor but a discussion in the work of the Cynic philosopher Teles explicitly states that the dead were removed from the space occupied by the living in order to ensure that they were refused entry into Hades.[55] In more cosmopolitan times the refusal of burial in one's home ground was looked upon with contempt by philosophers, as indeed appears from the writings of Teles, Epictetus (Arrian *Epicteti Dissertationes* 4.7.31), and the famous Cynic Diogenes who, according to one tradition, even wanted to be thrown forth after his death.[56]

A proper funeral in one's own area, then, was thought to be necessary for the final transition from the community of the living to Hades.[57] As such, the funeral is part of the larger complex of funeral rites which, in turn, belong to the general complex of the rites of passage, as has been demonstrated by Arnold van Gennep. This French folklorist and anthropologist showed that the changes an individual undergoes in his life cycle at birth, puberty, marriage, or death, in status such as becoming a priest or a king, in activity such as war, or in location, are often accomplished according to a set pattern. First there is a rite of separation, then a liminal period, and finally a rite of incorporation. The funeral rites belong to the rites of incorporation: they help the transition of the dead from the community of the living to the underworld, and, especially, the transition of the liv-

[55] For fear of pollution, see the important discussion by R. Parker, *Miasma* (Oxford 1983) ch. 2; Teles p. 29 Hense.

[56] Teles p. 29f. Hense; for Diogenes, see Diogenes *Epistulae* 25; Cicero *Tusculanae Disputationes* 1.104; Diogenes Laertius 6.79; Stobaeus *Anthologium*, ed. O. Hense, vol. 5 (Berlin 1894) 1119.

[57] This will explain the many cenotaphs, see D. Kurtz and J. Boardman, *Greek Burial Customs* (London 1971) 257-259 and passim.

ing to the new situation after the departure of one of their members.[58]

In rites of passage there is also often an element of delay and resistance. Society and/or the individual has, or pretends to have, great difficulty in changing status or position: in some countries bridegrooms used to hide away before being dragged by their friends to the wedding ceremony, people would only hand over the dead body of a beloved to the undertakers after a token resistance, and even today people who are offered an important position usually refuse first—only to accept eagerly afterwards.[59]

We find such an element of delay in the case of the soul. The soul changes from being part of a living body to being incorporated into Hades. In Homer this process is not particularly marked but we have seen that the transition takes place only after the funeral rites proper were completed, that is to say after some days. Between the separation from the body and the incorporation into Hades the soul remained briefly in a liminal state: it was neither part of the world of the living nor part of the world of the dead. Hertz also noted that the soul did not begin an afterlife immediately after death; in Oceania, for example, the soul is often believed to stay near the body for a while.[60] The same belief apparently also occurred in Archaic Greece for on black-figured vases of the end of the sixth century Patroclus' soul in the shape of an armored homunculus (the word *psychē* is actually written near the homunculus) is pictured near his

[58] A. van Gennep, *Les rites de passage* (Paris 1909), English ed., *The Rites of Passage*, trans. M. Vizedom and G. L. Caffee (Chicago and London 1960).

[59] For these and other examples of delay and resistance, see Bremmer, in M. J. Vermaseren (ed.), *Studies in Hellenistic Religions* (Leiden 1979) 9-22.

[60] Hertz, *Death and the Right Hand*, 34-37; Fischer, *Studien über Seelenvorstellungen*, 287.

dead body, and on the white *lekythoi* these often winged souls are pictured near the bier or the tomb, although usually not displaying the characteristic features of the deceased.[61] The bereaved evidently could not accept that the soul of the deceased would go to Hades immediately: there had to be some delay in the transition.

The function of the funeral rites in facilitating the transition of the soul also helps explain the difference between inhumation and cremation among the Greeks. The Greeks used the means of disposal of the dead to differentiate between people according to their status: suicides, children, adolescents, and slaves were often buried and not cremated, which was the normal way of disposal. Concomitant with this differentiation went an infranormal status for these categories in Hades, although people who died an untimely death sometimes occupied a supranormal position.

In the nineteenth and early twentieth centuries scholars attached especially great importance to the difference between cremation and burial.[62] Each practice was thought to correspond to a different idea about an afterlife, even though written sources did not support this view. Anthropological research has shown that among the North Amer-

[61] For Patroclus' soul, see K. P. Staehler, *Grab und Psyche des Patroklos* (Münster 1967); W. Felten, *Attische Unterweltsdarstellungen des VI. und V. Jh. v. Chr.* (Munich 1975) 42f. For the souls on the *lekythoi*, see Nilsson, *Geschichte*, 194-197; Felten, *Attische Unterweltsdarstellungen*, 42-45. For souls being winged, see Hultkrantz, *Conceptions of the soul*, 267: "There is nothing strange about the notion that a fugitive, delicate free-soul should assume the shape of a bird or other winged being. It may be presumed that peculiar dream-experiences—e.g. the sensation of hovering or flying— have stimulated the development of this popular conception." See more recently F. Cumont, *Recherches sur le symbolisme funéraire des Romains* (Paris 1942) 108-111 and *Lux perpetua* (Paris 1949) 293-297; J. Daniélou, "La colombe et la ténèbre dans la mystique byzantine," *Eranos Jahrbuch* 23 (1954) 389-418; P. Courcelle, "Flügel," in T. Klauser (ed.), *Reallexikon für Antike und Christentum*, vol. 8 (1972) 29-65.

[62] This is still done by Schnaufer, *Frühgriechischer Totenglaube*, 34-57.

ican Indians in California and elsewhere the two methods of disposal of the body have coexisted in the same tribe, and that the same method has held a different significance in different tribes.[63] In the Roman empire, too, cremation and burial coexisted, and succeeded each other without any corresponding change in ideas about the afterlife. In this respect the Romans were not unique among the Indo-European peoples, and there is now overwhelming evidence from all parts of the world that the presence or absence of burial, the change from burial to cremation and vice versa, or the gifts of burial goods, do not in themselves indicate beliefs in an afterlife. As Nock has observed, commenting on Epicurus, who denied the afterlife but provided for perpetual offerings for his immediate family: "Funerarary ritual is associated in the main with the tomb and not with afterlife as theoretically conceived."[64]

Even though, then, the relevance of contrasting inhumation and cremation *per se* has to be rejected, it would have been strange if the Greeks, with their polar way of thinking,[65] had not used the two modes of disposal to differentiate between people according to their age and the manner of their death. Indeed literary and archeological data testify to such a practice. Our earliest example of such

[63] A. L. Kroeber, "Disposal of the Dead," *American Anthropologist* 29 (1927) 308-315.

[64] A. D. Nock, *Essays on Religion and the Ancient World*, ed. Z. Stewart, 2 vols. (Oxford 1972) 1: 277-307 (the chapter was first published in 1932); W. A. van Es, *Grafritueel en kerstening* (Bussum 1968); G. Dumézil, *La religion romaine archaïque*, 2nd ed. (Paris 1974) 79f.; P. J. Ucko, "Ethnography and archeological interpretation of funerary remains," *World Archeology* 1 (1969) 262-280, who is followed by Kurtz and Boardman, *Greek Burial Customs*, 329. For Epicurus, see Nock, *Essays*, 287f.

[65] See B. A. van Groningen, *De antithese als Griekse denkvorm*, Mededelingen van de Koninklijke Vlaamse Academie voor Wetenschap, Letteren en Schone Kunsten van België, vol. 15, pt. 1 (Brussels 1953); G.E.R. Lloyd, *Polarity and Analogy* (Cambridge 1966).

a differentiation is the case of Ajax who, after his suicide, was not cremated but inhumed. According to the *Ilias Parva* this happened "because of the anger of the king," but it may well be wondered if that is not a later explanation, since suicides belonged to the class of the "dead without status" (below).[66] Suicides did not receive any honor in Thebes, and in Cyprus they had to be thrown unburied over the borders according to the laws of Demonassa.[67] In Athens one of their hands was cut off (Aeschines 3.244), and Plato, in his *Laws* (873 D), allowed suicides a burial only on the boundaries between the twelve districts, meaning on a piece of land falling outside the ordered, social world.[68]

Archeological data reveal that the same opposition could already be found around 700 B.C. in contemporary Eretrian graves, where a clear distinction existed between cremated adults and inhumed children and adolescents. This distinction must have corresponded with the social status of the deceased: only people with the proper civil status were cremated.[69]

This practice is not surprising for children. Nearly everywhere in the world the bodies of dead children have been disposed of in a simple or often careless way.[70] However,

[66] T. Allen, *Homeri opera*, vol. 5 (Oxford 1912) 130.

[67] For Thebes, see Zenobius 6.17 and O. Crusius, in *Corpus paroemiographorum Graecorum*, supp. (Hildesheim 1961) 5: 92-95. For Cyprus, see Dio Chrysostomus 64.3.

[68] In ancient Ireland unbaptized children used to be buried in boundary fences, see A. Rees and B. Rees, *Celtic Heritage*, 2nd ed. (London 1973) 94. For the liminality of boundaries, see E. Leach, *Culture and Communication* (Cambridge 1976) 33-36.

[69] C. Bérard, *L'Herôon à la porte de l'ouest* (Bern 1970) 48-53; also see L. Laurenzi, *Clara Rhodos* 8 (1936) 12; M. Gras, *Kokalos* 21 (1975) 49; P. Vidal-Naquet, *Le Chassseur noir* (Paris 1981) 189-191.

[70] Many examples can be found in M. Küsters, "Das Grab der Afrikaner," *Anthropos* 14-15 (1919-20) 639-728 and 16-17 (1921-22) 183-229, 913-959; E. Doerr, "Die Bestattungsformen in Ozeanien," *Anthropos* 30 (1935) 369-420, 727-765; F. Speiser, "Über die Totenbestattung in Insel Mela-

this does not occur universally.[71] Aristotle mentions that on the isle of Keos children were mourned for one year, and from the excavations it appears that great care was lavished on the young Eretrian dead, a care for which some Paleolithic graves of young children are silent witnesses.[72] Nor were children always inhumed. Especially in Athens and the surrounding districts there is much evidence for the cremation of children.[73] The differences in practice suggest varying degrees of affection on the part of the parents or varying economic circumstances for the family. Some scholars want to explain the inhumation of babies by the idea of rebirth;[74] however, this is hardly probable. Since a simple inhumation without the accompanying idea of rebirth is often found, the idea of rebirth for ancient Greece cannot be inferred without direct statements from our sources. Nilsson observed that the inhumation of children went together with the near absence of funeral gifts.[75] This arche-

---

nesien," *Internationales Archiv für Ethnographie* 40 (1942) 125-173; W. Stöhr, *Das Totenritual der Dajak* (Cologne 1954) passim; W. Déonna, "Cimétières de bébés," *Revue archéologique de l'Est et du Centre-Est* 6 (1955) 231-247; I. Schwidetsky, "Sonderbestattungen und ihre paläodemographische Bedeutung," *Homo* 16 (1966) 230-247, esp. 233-237 (much material).

[71] Nilsson, *Geschichte*, 175 is certainly too sweeping on this point.

[72] Aristotle fragment 611, 28 Rose. For Eretria, see Bérard, *L'Heröon*, 52. For Paleolithic graves, see H. Müller-Karpe, *Handbuch der Vorgeschichte*, vol. 1 (Munich 1966) 169.

[73] *Praktika tes Archaiologikes Etaireias* 1951, 123 (probably) and 1953, 92; R. S. Young, "Sepulturae intra urbem," *Hesperia* 20 (1951) 67-134; *Praktika* 1961, 5; *Archaiologikon Deltion* 20 (1965) B 40; *Athenische Mitteilungen* 81 (1966) 14f. J. Rudhardt, "Sur quelques bûchers d'enfants découverts dans la ville d'Athènes," *Museum Helveticum* 20 (1963) 10-20 unnecessarily suggests that the cremation of the children was for purificatory reasons.

[74] A. Dieterich, *Mutter Erde*, 3rd ed. (Leipzig 1925); M. Eliade, *Traité de l'histoire des religions*, 2nd ed. (Paris 1953) 217-219; Bérard, *L'Heröon*, 52.

[75] Nilsson, *Geschichte*, 175. As especially Stöhr, *Das Totenritual der*

ological evidence indicates that for children a proper funeral with all the accompanying rites was absent but that the body was properly disposed of.[76] Dead children were treated similarly in ancient Rome. Children less than forty days old were buried in a niche in the wall of the house; they were not cremated unless they had reached the age when their teeth had come through.[77]

A special burial for the adolescent is much more surprising. Adolescents who died during their initiation were often buried in a secret way, and the same custom may once have existed in ancient Greece. In Ilion two maidens of the best families of Locri had to spend one year in the temple of Athena Ilias. During this period they were barefoot, their hair was cut short, they had only one dress to wear, and they had to keep the temple clean. Even though this ritual is not an initiation proper, its closest parallels are the puberty rituals, and it is most easily understood as a transformation of a former tribal initiation. When one of these maidens happened to die during the year she had to be buried in

---

Dajak, has stressed, the manner of disposal, whether cremation or burial, only forms part of a greater complex, and it has been the great mistake of Rohde and others to isolate one detail, an approach that does not at all do justice to the function of the funeral rites as a whole.

[76] Plutarch *Moralia* 612 A, B states that according to the "ancestral and ancient usages and laws" funeral rites are absent for children. Unfortunately, we do not know anything about the precise content or age of these laws, but it does not seem improbable that the usage goes back to the Archaic Age.

[77] For Rome, see J. E. King, "Infant Burial," *Classical Review* 17 (1903) 83f.; H. J. Rose, "Nocturnal Funerals in Rome," *Classical Quarterly* 17 (1923) 191-194; Onians, *The Origins of European Thought*, 263f.; Déonna, "Cimétières de bébés," 234-237; H. Wagenvoort, *Studies in Roman Literature, Culture and Religion* (Leiden 1956) 93-96; J. ter Vrugt-Lenz, *Mors immatura* (Diss. Univ. of Leiden 1960) 63-67; P. Boyancé, *Etudes sur la religion romaine* (Rome 1972) 73-89. For the burial in the wall, see Fulgentius *Expositio sermonum antiquorum* 560.7. For teeth, see Pliny *Natural History* 7.15.

secrecy. Does this special burial during the initiation explain the evidence for adolescent burial? The sources do not give a definite answer to this question but in Rome too the adolescent was buried in the same way as the child.[78]

If children and adolescents are seen as people without a full place in the community, it will not be surprising to find that their disposal strongly resembled those of slaves.[79] It is true that, at least in Athens, the master had the obligation to dispose of his dead slave ([Demosthenes] 43.58), but we hear of no funeral rites.[80] This separation between free citizens and slaves is also evident in the treatment of those who had fallen at Marathon, where the slaves who had been released before the battle were not buried in the same grave as the free Athenians but together with the Plataeans (Pausanias 10.20.2). Moreover, they were buried and not cremated, which was by far the cheaper method. Similarly, the Spartans buried their dead separately from the Helots after the battle at Plataea (Herodotus 9.85). And when we hear of released slaves and free men buried together on the Kerameikos (Pausanias 1.29.7), it is not certain that they were buried in the same grave.[81]

---

[78] For the Locrian maidens, see F. Graf, "Die lokrischen Mädchen," *Studi Storico-Religiosi* 2 (1978) 61-79. For the ethnological evidence, see A. Brelich, *Paides e parthenoi* (Rome 1969) 60 n. 29. For Rome, see Tacitus *Annales* 13.17.2 (Brittannicus); Servius *Aeneis* 11.143.

[79] See the extensive discussion by F. Bömer, *Untersuchungen über die Religion der Sklaven in Griechenland und Rom*, vol. 4, Abhandlungen der Akademie der Wissenschaften und der Literatur in Mainz, Geistes- und sozialwissenschaftliche Klasse 1963, no. 10 (Wiesbaden 1963) 138-157. For ethnological evidence, see Schwidetzky, "Sonderbestattungen," 241-243.

[80] It was a religious duty to bury the dead (Scholia on Sophocles *Antigone* 255) for the corpse was impure, see now Parker, *Miasma*, ch. 2.

[81] For Marathon, see Pausanias 1.32.3; Bömer, *Untersuchungen*, 4: 132f.; K. W. Welwei, *Unfreie im antiken Kriegsdienst*, vol. 1 (Wiesbaden 1974) 27f. For Kerameikos, see Welwei, ibidem, 41.

Since one of the functions of the funeral rites was to help the transition of the soul into the afterlife, it may be reasonably assumed that such a transition did not take place fully in the case of suicides, slaves, children, and adolescents. Unfortunately we have no explicit data for the first two categories in the period under investigation, but it may well be that the refusal of Charon to ferry over the slave Xanthias in Aristophanes' comedy *The Frogs* (190f.) is due to this idea about the slave's position after death.[82] For children and adolescents, however, there are clearer indications that their souls did not receive a normal status in the afterlife.

There is widespread evidence that children, adolescents, and others who died an untimely death have a special status after death. Because of their abnormal death they have been thought to roam about as revenants, become vampires, or have an inferior position in an afterlife.[83] In Africa those who die prematurely or violently, who are killed in war, by accident or by their own hand, and those to whom a funeral has been denied are all considered to die an abnormal death. The same categories exist in Indonesia as in Africa, but with the addition of those who have died of a particularly grave disease, and the unknown dead. In Western Europe the untimely dead also have a special status and have become incorporated into the *arme Seelen*; and in modern Greece they become the *vrikolakes*, the revenants, although

[82] Bömer *Untersuchungen*, 4: 153.

[83] Hertz, *Death and the Right Hand*, 85; L. Lévy-Bruhl, *La mentalité primitive*, 2nd ed. (Paris 1922) 310; A. E. Jensen, *Mythos und Kult bei Naturvölkern* (Wiesbaden 1951) 382-388; J. Cazeneuve, *Sociologie du rite* (Paris 1971) 141f. J. Pentikäinen, "The Dead without Status," *Temenos* 4 (1969) 92-102 has even called these particular cases the "dead without status" but that is a less well-chosen term, since the untimely dead sometimes occupy a higher place in the afterworld than the normal dead.

enriched with the impious, bad mayors, and custom offi-
cers.[84]

There are some indications that the souls of those who
died an untimely (*ahōroi*) or violent death (*biaiothanatoi*)
in ancient Greece were supposed by some people, but certainly not all, to have had a different fate from those who
had died a normal death.[85] In the Archaic period, too, there
are traces of such a separate fate. For the souls of children
this is apparent from the traditions surrounding the Lesbian
Gello, since she was supposed to have died in childhood
and then to have become a ghost who frightened children.[86]
Gello is related to bogies such as Akko, Alphito (Plutarch

---

[84] For Africa, see L.-V. Thomas, *Anthropologie de la mort* (Paris 1975)
310; V. Bendl, "Die Bedeutung des 'schlimmen Todes' bei den Ewe, Ghana,"
Wiener Völkerkundliche Mitteilungen 21-22 (1979-80) 57-82; for Indonesia, see H. J. Sell, *Der schlimme Tod bei den Völkern Indonesiens* (The
Hague 1955); for western Europe, see O. Mengis, "Arme Seelen," in Bächtold-Stäubli (ed.), *Handwörterbuch der deutschen Aberglaube*, vol. 1 (1927)
584-597; M. Haavio, " 'A running stream they dare na cross,' " *Studia
Fennica* 8 (1959) 125-142; E. Moser-Rath, "Arme Seelen," in W. Peuckert
(ed.), *Handwörterbuch der Sage*, vol. 1 (Göttingen 1962) 628-641; L. Pauli,
Keltischer Volksglaube (Munich 1975); for modern Greece, see R. Blum
and E. Blum, *The Dangerous Hour* (London 1970) 70-76; T. Vlachos,
"Geister- und Dämonenvorstellungen im Südosteuropäischen Raum grie-
chischer Sprachzugehörigkeit," *Österreichische Zeitschrift für Volkskunde* 25 (1971) 217-248, esp. 228f.

[85] F. Cumont, *Afterlife in Roman Paganism* (New Haven 1922) 128-
147 and *Lux perpetua*, 303-342; J. H. Waszink, "Biothanati," in Klauser
(ed.), *Reallexikon für Antike und Christentum*, vol. 2 (1954) 391-394; Ter
Vrugt-Lenz, *Mors immatura*; Lattimore, *Themes*, 186; E. Griessmair, *Das
Motiv der Mors immatura in den griechischen metrischen Grabinschriften*
(Innsbruck 1966) 28-38; T. Hopfner, *Griechisch-Ägyptischer
Offenbarungszauber*, 2nd ed., vol. 1 (Amsterdam 1974) 177-188; A.-M.
Vérilhac, Παῖδες ἄωροι, vol. 1 (Athens 1978).

[86] Roscher, *Ausführliches mythologisches Lexikon*, vol. 1 (1884) 1610;
P. Maas, *Byzantinische Zeitschrift* 17 (1908) 224f.; H. Hepding, *Hessische
Blätter für Volkskunde* 23 (1924) 119-125; D. B. Oeconomides, "Yello
dans les traditions des peuples Hellénique et Roumain," *IV International
Congress for Folk Narrative Research in Athens* (Athens 1965) 328-334;
Herter, *Kleine Schriften*, 50f.

Moralia 1040 B), and Mormo, bogies, like masks (!), used by the Greeks, who of course did not yet have a Benjamin Spock, to frighten children.[87] Following Von Sydow we may call these bogies "ficts" because they do not belong to the world of adult belief.[88] Rites, myths, and memorates connected with them do not exist. They have been explained as spirits with a diminished status but there is no evidence for a former higher status, and it should be remembered that the situations which cause the mentioning of ficts—children being naughty or careless—always exist, even when there are no such spirits.[89] It does seem, however, that Gello is not identical with these bogies since the content of her traditions—when and where we are able to reach a more precise idea about them, and it is only possible to do this from the Byzantine Age onwards—is much richer; a different fate in a somewhat later period can most probably also be inferred from the remark of Er (Plato *Republic* 615 C) that "about those who had just been born and lived but a short time he related other things not worth mentioning."

The special fate for the souls of adolescents is revealed in a passage in the *Odyssey* relating Odysseus' visit to the underworld. The first person to speak to Odysseus was El-

[87] For Akko, see Roscher, *Ausführliches mythologisches Lexikon*, 1 (1884) 210f.; L. Robert, *Monnaies grecques* (Geneva 1967) 119-123; J. Strubbe, *Beiträge zur Namenkunde* 13 (1978) 378f. For Mormo, see Roscher, *Ausführliches mythologisches Lexikon*, vol. 2, pt. 2 (1894-97) 3213; L. Robert, *Monnaies antiques en Troade* (Paris 1966) 119f.; Herter, *Kleine Schriften*, 50; M. L. West, ZPE 25 (1977) 107. For masks, see Plutarch *Moralia* 600 E; Arrian *Epicteti dissertationes* 2.1.15, 3.22.106; Dio Chrysostomus 5.17, 66.20; Timaeus *Lexicon Platonicum* s.v. *mormolukeion*.

[88] C. W. von Sydow, *Selected Papers on Folklore* (Copenhagen 1948) 79-84; but also see M. Kuusi, *Regen bei Sonnenschein* (Helsinki 1957) 371f.

[89] Against Nilsson, *Geschichte*, 226 and G. Binder, in Klauser (ed.), *Reallexikon für Antike und Christentum* 9 (1976) 84. See R. Kvideland, "Barnetru," in B. af Klintberg et al. (eds.), *Studier tillägnade Carl-Herman Tillhagen* (Lund 1976) 233-254; L. Honko, *Geisterglaube in Ingermanland*, vol. 1 (Helsinki 1962) 132.

penor, who was still unburied at the time. Since he had not yet been properly buried he still belonged to the special category of the abnormal dead, but before him Odysseus saw:

Brides and youths unwed, and old men of many and evil days,
and tender maidens with grief yet fresh at heart;
and many there were, wounded with bronze-shod spears,
men slain in fight with their bloody mail about them[90]

The persons here enumerated, as has repeatedly been observed, exactly fit the categories of *ahōroi* and *biaiothanatoi*.[91] The only category we have not yet met are the old people, but they also belong to those who are often buried without any ritual.[92] In ancient Greece there existed traditions about a voluntary suicide of old people, a practice that points to the custom of eliminating the aged. This custom was once widespread outside and, probably, inside Europe,[93] and the Greeks ascribed it to the Trogodytes (Diodorus Siculus 3.33.5), Tibarenoi (Porphyrius *On Abstinence* 4.21), Hyrcanians (ibidem), Scythians (ibidem), Heruli (Procopius *The Gothic Wars* 2.14), Bactrians (Onesikritus by Strabo 11.11.3) Sogdians (Plutarch *Moralia* 328 C), Der-

---

[90] *Odyssey* 11.38-41, tr. S. H. Butcher and A. Lang, *The Odyssey of Homer*, 3rd ed. (London 1887).

[91] Lattimore, *Themes*, 187; R. Merkelbach, *Untersuchungen zu Odyssee*, 2nd ed. (Munich 1969) 189; K. Meuli, *Gesammelte Schriften*, 2 vols. (Basel and Stuttgart 1975) 1: 316. Zenodotus, Aristophanes, and Aristarchus rejected the passage on the grounds of inconsistency with what follows, but Van Leeuwen (ad locum) rightly calls this objection "inane crimen."

[92] Hertz, *Death and the Right Hand*, 85; Schwidetzky, "Sonderbestattungen," 237f.

[93] See more recently K. E. Müller, "Zur Frage der Altentötung im westeurasiatischen Raum," *Paideuma* 14 (1968) 17-44; M. Gavazzi, "The Tradition of killing Old People," in L. Dégh et al. (eds.), *Folklore Today: A Festschrift for Richard M. Dorson* (Bloomington 1976) 175-180; E. Moser-Rath, "Altentötung," in K. Ranke (ed.), *Enzyklopädie des Märchens*, vol. 1 (Berlin 1977) 388-395 (with older bibliography).

bices (Strabo 11.11.8), and Massagetes (Herodotus 1.216; Strabo 11.8.6); in the case of the latter two peoples the killing was even coupled with endocannibalism, this too being a not uncommon practice.[94] The historical truth of the matter cannot be ascertained and we must make allowance for the tendency of the Greeks to ascribe to the peoples surrounding them a certain degree of primitive behavior to contrast them unfavorably with themselves.[95] For Greece itself, these traditions all circle around the isle of Keos, but there are some legends collected in modern times on the mainland suggesting that this custom was once perhaps more widely practiced than appears from the historical sources.[96]

Since, then, these persons were the first to be met in the underworld by Odysseus, at one time they may have been believed to reside at the outskirts of the underworld without actually entering it, and so to form a special category of the dead with an infranormal status.[97]

[94] H. Becker, "Die endokannibalistischen Riten als früheste Erscheinungsform der Anthropophagie," *Zeitschrift für Ethnologie* 92 (1967) 248-253. Strabo 4.5.4 ascribes the practice to the inhabitants of Ierne. However, the recent controversy about cannibalism warns us against an all too ready acceptance of these reports, see W. Arens, *The Man-Eating Myth: Anthropology and Anthropophagy* (New York 1979); P. Vidal-Naquet, *Les juifs, la mémoire et le présent* (Paris 1981) 197ff.

[95] See S. Pembroke, "Women in Charge: the Function of Alternatives in Early Greek Tradition and the Ancient Idea of Matriarchy," *Journal of the Warburg and Courtauld Institutes* 39 (1967) 1-36; I. Chirassi-Colombo, "The role of Thrace in Greek Religion," *Thracia* 2 (1974) 71-80; M. Detienne, *Dionysos mis à mort* (Paris 1977) 133-160; F. Hartog, *Le miroir d'Hérodote* (Paris 1980); C. Segal, *Tragedy and Civilization* (Cambridge, Mass. 1981) 29f.

[96] Aristotle fragment 611.29 Rose; Menander fragment 797 Koerte; Theophrastus *Historia plantarum* 9.16.9; Meleagros *Anthologia Graeca* 7.470; Strabo 10.5.6; Aelian *Varia Historia* 3.37; Stobaeus *Anthologium*, ed. O. Hense, vol. 3, (Berlin 1894) 325f. For modern legends, see G. A. Megas, *Laographia* 25 (1967) 207-216.

[97] P. von der Mühll, *Ausgewählte kleine Schriften* (Basel 1975) 25 as-

Warriors, too, had a special fate in post-Homeric times. According to Heraclitus, "Gods and man honour those slain in battle" which "most probably alludes to a posthumous or eschatological reward by gods of those slain in battle."[98] The warriors who fell at Marathon were worshipped as heroes, as were those who fell at Plataea.[99] This heroization assured them a supranormal status in contrast with the infranormal one in the *Odyssey* (above).

The warriors were not the only ones with a special fate. In ancient Greece there are other examples of *ahōroi* and *biaiothanatoi* being elevated to a higher status. The worship of the well-known heroes constitutes a different problem, even though they also often died an untimely death.[100] Greek

---

cribes 11.38-41 to a Katabasis of Heracles and wonders: "deutet nicht die Parallele in Vergil 6, 306ff. darauf, dass sie (these verses)—ähnlich wie ja auch im λ(Odyssey 11)—beim Eintritt des Herakles in die Unterwelt im Unterweltsgedicht standen." The idea that the untimely dead have to remain at the outskirts of the underworld also occurs in a Smyrnean epigram published by I. Hendriks, *ZPE* 40 (1980) 200-205, reprinted in G. Petzl, *Die Inschriften von Smyrna*, vol. 1 (Bonn 1982) no. 550.

[98] Heraclitus B 24 Diels/Kranz, fragment 96a Marcovich, and fragment 100 Kahn; Marcovich, ibidem, 510.

[99] For Marathon, see Pausanias 1.32.4; *Inscriptiones Graecae* 2nd ed., vol. 2 1006, 69ff. For Plataea, see Thucydides 3.58; Plutarch *Aristides* 21; M. P. Nilsson, *Griechische Feste* (Leipzig 1906) 455f.; N. Loraux, *L'Invention d'Athènes* (Paris 1981) 39-41. Other examples: Nilsson, *Geschichte*, 718; F. Sokolowski, *Lois sacrées des cités grecques, Supplément* (Paris 1962) 64; *Nouveaux choix d'inscriptions grecques* (Paris 1971) 19; *Inscriptiones Creticae*, vol. 3, IV.38 (probably); Bernand, *Inscriptions métriques*, 4.6.

[100] This worship has often been discussed, see, most recently, J. N. Coldstream, "Hero-cults in the Age of Homer," *Journal of Hellenic Studies* 96 (1976) 8-17; Burkert, *Griechische Religion*, 312-319; M. L. West, *Hesiod: Works and Days* (Oxford 1978) 370-373; C. Bérard, "Récupérer la mort du prince: Héroisation et formation de la cité," in G. Gnoli and J.-P. Vernant (eds.), *La mort, les morts dans les sociétés anciennes* (Cambridge and Paris 1982) 89-105; A. Snodgrass, "Les origines du culte des héros dans la Grèce antique," ibidem, 107-119. For the untimely death, see A. Brelich, *Gli eroi greci* (Rome 1958) 90.

mythology records a number of cases of people who were killed by lightning and, subsequently, honored as gods or heroes, although there are many other peoples who consider those killed by lightning as having an infranormal status.[101] Near Epidaurus was the grave of the heroine Hyrnetho who was killed during a pregnancy (Pausanias 2.28.3). Near Arcadian Kaphyai was a temple of Artemis where each year offerings were burnt for children who according to the myth had been killed unjustly (Pausanias 8.23.7). The dead suitors of Hippodameia were buried by Oenomaos without much ado but Pelops later made sacrifices to them as heroes (Pausanias 6.21.9-11).

In Lucanian Temesa, according to the legend, the inhabitants had stoned to death one of Odysseus' sailors who had violated one of their virgins. Since Odysseus did not care for him—which must mean that he did not perform the proper funeral rites—the ghost of the sailor wandered and did not come to rest until after the people of Temesa had set apart an area of sacred ground for him and built a temple. Besides this they had to give him, each year, the most beautiful virgin. All this clearly implies an elevation to a higher plane for the dead sailor. The story is not yet finished, however; the ritual of sacrificing a virgin was stopped by the Olympian victor Euthymos who defeated the ghost of the hero in a fight after which he, naturally, married the

[101] E. Rohde, *Psyche*, 2nd ed., 2 vols. (Freiburg and Berlin 1898) 1: 320-322; H. Usener, *Kleine Schriften*, vol. 4 (Leipzig and Berlin 1913) 478f.; A. B. Cook, *Zeus*, vol. 2, pt. 2 (Cambridge 1925) 22-29; Burkert, *Glotta* 39 (1961) 308; Nilsson, *Geschichte*, 72; G. Zuntz, *Persephone* (Oxford 1971) 316. In Greece anyone struck by lightning was buried and not cremated (Artemidorus 2.9). According to Plutarch *Moralia* 665 C they were not buried at all. Among the Romans cremation, the normal way of burial, was forbidden them (Pliny *Natural History* 2.145). For infranormal status, see J. Cazeneuve, *Les rites et la condition humaine* (Paris 1957) 149f.

girl (Pausanias 6.6.7-11). At the end of his life Euthymos simply disappeared and was worshipped as a hero. Here, too, the abnormal death is clearly connected with heroization.[102]

With Euthymos we have reached more historical times. Here the best example is Kleomedes. This great athlete caused the death of a number of children in his town of Astypalaea. Because the Astypalaeans were trying to catch him, he hid in a chest in the temple of Athena; when the chest was finally opened no one was found, and Kleomedes was subsequently honored as a hero.[103] Not only did the absence of a body cause such an honor. The inhabitants of Amathus had to sacrifice to Onesilus as a hero after a bee swarm had settled in his skull, which they had hung up at the gates (Herodotus 5.114); and in Cyprus, during a famine, the gods ordered the inhabitants of Kition to pay honor to Cimon who, according to some, had died of wounds during the siege of that town (Plutarch *Cimon* 19). Is not the most plausible explanation in these last two cases also, that something about their death caused these unnatural things to happen?[104]

A supranormal status, then, for the abnormal dead is not

---

[102] See G. Gianelli, *Culti e miti della Magna Grecia*, 2nd ed. (Florence 1963) 223-235; Callimachus fragment 98 Pfeiffer. Heroization: Pausanias 6.6.10; Aelian *Varia Historia* 8.18; Callimachus fragment 99 Pfeiffer mentions sacrifices to Euthymos during his life time. The legend is the subject of a Dutch novel: S. Vestdijk, *De held van Temesa* (The Hague and Rotterdam 1962).

[103] Plutarch *Romulus* 28; Pausanias 6.9.6-8; Origen *Contra Celsum* 3.25, 33; Eusebius *Praeparatio evangelica* 5.34.2; Suidas s.v. *Kleomedes*.

[104] Compare also Herodotus (2.90; also see Aelian *De natura animalium* 10.21) who records that in Egypt the bodies of those who were drowned or caught by crocodiles were considered to be supranormal ones and therefore received the best possible funeral, see A. Bataille, *Memnonia* (Cairo 1952) 59f. (with older bibliography); J. Quaegebeur, ZPE 24 (1977) 246-250; R. A. Wild, *Water in the Cultic Worship of Isis and Sarapis* (Leiden 1981) 90f.

uncommon. Hertz had already noted the ambiguous position of the abnormal dead and observed that they became either elect or damned.[105] To judge from the literary and archeological evidence it seems, however, that in the period under investigation deceased children and adolescents usually received an infranormal status and consequently were not normally given the full funeral rites accorded the normal dead and were thought to remain as souls outside or at the outskirts of the world of the dead.

A Return of the Dead?

In the Archaic period revenants and ghosts are virtually unheard of, although somewhat later Plato (*Phaedrus* 81 C, D) mentions the existence of ghosts wandering around tombs and graveyards.[106] The reason for this near-absence may be due to the fragmentary state of our sources, but one cannot exclude the possibility that the belief in ghosts was stronger on the mainland than in Ionia and the Greek islands, the area from which the greater part of our earliest sources derive. In these areas emigration from the mainland may well have had a diminishing influence on the role ascribed to ancestors and, consequently, to ghosts.[107]

[105] Hertz, *Death and the Right Hand*, 153 n. 339; J. Bayet, *Croyances et rites dans la Rome antique* (Paris 1971) 133f. Burkert, *Griechische Religion*, 305 observes regarding death through lightning: "Blitztod ist Vernichtung und Erwählung zugleich."; similarly W. Speyer, *Antike und Abendland* 24 (1978) 59f. and in Klauser (ed.), *Reallexikon für Antike und Christentum*, vol. 10 (1978) 1124-1127.

[106] Nilsson, *Geschichte*, 182-184; Burkert, *Griechische Religion*, 300, 317. The tradition of Plato's passage is followed by P. Courcelle, "L'âme au tombeau," in *Mélanges d'histoire des religions offerts à Henri-Charles Puech* (Paris 1974) 331-336.

[107] For the connection between the importance ascribed to ancestors and the belief in ghosts, see K. Thomas, *Religion and the Decline of Magic*, 2nd ed. (Harmondsworth 1973) 701-724.

Considering this near-absence of testimonia, we will restrict ourselves to a discussion of the problem of whether the Archaic Age Greeks believed ghosts appeared during the Athenian festival of the Anthesteria. Since this festival was common to Athens and the Ionians, it must reach back into the period before the Ionian emigration. Some scholars have thought that the proverb "Out of the door, you Kares, the Anthesteria are over" (Zenobius 4.33) originated to expel the spirits of the dead, who appeared within the city during the celebrations. Although in some societies the topsy turvy nature of ceremonies like the Anthesteria is associated with a return of the dead, this festival recalled for its participants, among other events, the threat of strangers who could destroy the social fabric. The proverb expressed this fear.[108]

The festival took place in the spring on the eleventh, twelfth, and thirteenth days of the month Anthesterion; it was dedicated to Dionysos and received its name from the flowering of the vine tendrils. On the first day, the Pithoigia, or "Jar-opening," the Athenians brought their new wine to the sanctuary of Dionysos of the Marshes where they mixed it with water, poured a libation to the gods, and took their first taste. After the grape harvest in the late summer the grape juice had been stored in earthenware jars for the fermenting process and the jars had been left unopened. In Greece wine mixed with water was the main drink of Greek males (wine was often forbidden to females) and

---

[108] For the Anthesteria, see L. Deubner, *Attische Feste* (Berlin 1932) 93-123; H. S. Versnel, *Triumphus* (Leiden 1970) 245-250 and "Destruction, Devotio and Despair," esp. 587-591; W. Burkert, *Homo necans, RGVV,* vol. 32 (Berlin and New York 1972) 236-273 and *Griechische Religion,* 358-364; H. W. Parke, *Festivals of the Athenians* (London 1977) 107-120. For the documentation of the individual items of the festival I refer the reader in general to Burkert, *Homo necans,* with his extensive notes and bibliography.

drinking wine played an important role in the most important gathering of Greek males, the symposium.[109] The Greeks even distinguished between themselves and neighboring peoples by ascribing to the neighbors the drinking of water or unmixed wine—the opposite of drinking mixed wine.[110]

Given the importance of wine for their way of life the Greeks must have anxiously awaited the day of the Pithoigia, and once the jars were opened they could relax and happily enjoy the wine. Such a relaxation also occurred after the harvest had changed a period of scarcity into one of plenty, and there is a large amount of ethnological evidence demonstrating that this relaxation, which usually manifested itself during first-fruit festivals, found expression in the consumption of large amounts of food and drink, and in a general suspension of the normal rules of society. Similarly in Western Europe, new wine was often consumed in large quantities on St. Martin's Day, a day which was in addition the scene of rites of reversal and the carrying of masks.[111]

This suspension of the normal social order is also perfectly illustrated by the second and central day of the festival called

[109] For the importance of wine, see Xenophon *Respublica Lacedaemoniorum* 1.3; Alkimos *FGrH* 560 F 2; Aelian *Varia Historia* 2.38; Athenaeus 10.429 A; also see F. Graf, "Milch, Honig und Wein," in G. Piccaluga (ed.), *Perennitas. Studi in onore di Angelo Brelich* (Rome 1980) 209-221, esp. 216; A. Henrichs, "Changing Dionysiac Identities," in B. F. Meyer (ed.), *Self-Definition in the Greco-Roman World* (London 1982). In Rome wine was also forbidden to women: G. Piccaluga, *Studi e Materiali di Storia delle Religioni* 35 (1964) 202-223. For the symposium, see J. Trumpf, "Über das Trinken in der Poesie des Alkaios," *ZPE* 12 (1973) 139-160; Von der Mühll, *Ausgewählte kleine Schriften*, 483-505; O. Murray, *Early Greece* (Brighton 1980) 197-203; Henrichs, "Changing Dionysiac Identities," § I.1.

[110] Graf, "Milch, Honig und Wein," 215; add Bremmer, *Arethusa* 13 (1980) 295 n. 49 and *ZPE* 39 (1980) 33.

[111] First fruit festivals: V. Lanternari, *La grande festa*, 2nd ed. (Bari 1976). St. Martin's Day: P. Sartori, *Sitte und Brauch*, vol. 3 (Leipzig 1914) 266; Meuli, *Gesammelte Schriften*, vol. 1, 155f.

Choes, or "Wine-jugs." It was considered an uncanny day; all the temples were closed with ropes, except for the sanctuary of Dionysos of the Marshes that was closed for the rest of the year. This meant that no oaths could be witnessed, no business transactions completed, no wedding ceremonies performed.[112] It was in agreement with the topsy turvy character of the feast that the priestesses of Dionysos' temple, the Gerarai, were probably older women in whom males normally had lost all interest.[113] Free men and slaves participated in the festival equally, and on that day even a misanthrope would feel obliged to dine with at least one other person.[114] Yet, "anarchy" was not total since the prohibition of wine for women was not lifted; it remained strictly the privilege of the Athenian males.[115]

The day started with the chewing of leaves of the buckthorn, a rather unappetizing plant, reputed to be good for warding off apparitions (*phantasmata*).[116] The scholars, who see the festival as a time when ghosts appear, always mention this quality of the plant, but in that case it is less clear why it was chewed only in the morning, whereas the ghosts supposedly roamed the city for the whole day. Burkert interprets the chewing more convincingly as a cathartic prep-

[112] Photios s.v. *miara hēmera*; Burkert, *Homo necans*, 242f.

[113] See Parke, *Festivals*, 112 and Versnel, "Destruction, *Devotio* and Despair," 590 n. 207 who illuminatingly compares the old priestess of the Roman Parentalia. For the position of old women, see W. K. Lacey, *The Family in Classical Greece* (London 1968) 175. Drunken old women were a favorite butt of the comedy, which seems to suggest that the prohibition of drinking wine was not strictly applied to elder women, see H. G. Oeri, *Der Typ der komischen Alten in der griechischen Komödie* (Basel 1948) 13-18, 39-46; J. W. Salomonsson, "Der Trunkenbold und die trunkene Alte," *Bulletin Antieke Beschaving* 55 (1980) 65-135.

[114] R. Pfeiffer on Callimachus fragment 178.2 (slaves); Plutarch *Antony* 70 (misanthrope).

[115] Against Versnel, "Destruction, *Devotio* and Despair," 590; see Burkert, *Homo necans*, 248; Henrichs, "Changing Dionysiac Identities," § I.1.

[116] Nicander *Theriaca* 861f. and Scholia on line 860.

aration for the great meal to come. Similarly, during first-fruit festivals elsewhere in the world, people started the day by swallowing bitter concoctions in order to purify themselves before they tasted the new food.[117] In the late afternoon the Athenians gathered for a banquet and drinking bout that was organized in such a way as to make it the exact opposite of a normal banquet. The guests brought their own food, except for the dessert, and the wine in their own jug; they were seated at separate tables instead of sharing couches. After a trumpet had given the starting sign each banqueteer tried to empty his jug as fast as possible, which must have been quite a feat, since a jug contained about three liters of wine! The drinking took place in complete silence, another contrast to the convivial nature of the symposium.

The silence has been interpreted as a sign of "communitas," a term introduced by Victor Turner for the bond that can originate in a liminal situation when the normal rules of society are absent, but society is not totally atomized.[118] Silence, like laughter, is a subject that has not yet received the attention it deserves, and "communitas" can sometimes be a helpful concept for its interpretation but not in this particular case.[119] According to Turner, the bonds of "com-

[117] J. G. Frazer, *Spirits of the Corn and of the Wild*, 3rd ed., vol. 3 (London 1912) 73, 75f. Burkert, *Homo necans*, 244 refers to these passages but—not surprisingly, if less convincingly in my opinion—opts for a derivation from hunting customs.

[118] Versnel, "Destruction, *Devotio* and Despair," 590. For "communitas," see V. Turner, *Dramas, Fields and Metaphors* (Ithaca and London 1974) 231-299.

[119] On silence, see O. Casel, *De veterum philosophorum silentio mystico*, *RGVV*, vol. 16 (Giessen 1919); G. Mensching, *Das heilige Schweigen*, *RGVV*, vol. 20 (Giessen 1925); K. H. Basso, "To give up on Words: Silence in Western Apache Culture," *Southwestern Journal of Anthropology* 26 (1970) 213-230; U. Ruberg, *Beredtes Schweigen in lehrhafter und erzählender deutscher Literatur des Mittelalters* (Munich 1978).

munitas" are "undifferentiated, egalitarian, direct, extant, nonrational, existential, I-Thou (in Buber's sense)."[120] It is hard to recognize those qualities in a group of Athenians trying to gulp down their wine as fast as possible.

The Athenians explained the strange nature of this drinking party by the arrival of Orestes in Athens on the eve of the Anthesteria before his purification from the murder of his mother Clytemnestra. The Athenian king feared that Orestes would pollute the other guests at the festival if he participated, but did not want to be inhospitable, and ordered therefore that all the temples should be closed and that all the guests should drink their wine at separate tables. In this way Orestes could still participate in the feast but would not contaminate the other guests. The myth explains the ritual by focusing on a marginal stranger; the same theme is also apparent in other myths connected with the festival.

A Greek proverb from the period also presents the theme of the marginal stranger: "Out of the door, you Kares, the Anthesteria are over" (Zenobius 4.33). Unfortunately, there is no certainty about the origin of the saying; in Greek it constitutes an iambic trimeter, and it seems reasonable therefore to assume that it derives from a comedy. However, whether the comedy adopted a ritual saying from the Anthesteria or whether the trimeter was afterwards introduced in some way into or connected with the festival seems equally possible. According to tradition the proverb was repeated whenever people became obtrusive and tried repeatedly to take liberties that had been permitted on only one occasion.[121] Tradition recounted that it was either originally said

---

[120] V. Turner, *Image and Pilgrimage in Christian Culture* (New York 1978) 250.

[121] Zenobius 4.33; Photios s.v. *thyradze Kares*; Suidas s.v. *thyradze Kares*, also in Pausanias (Gr.) θ 20 Erbse.

to Carian slaves who had not yet gone back to work after the festival was over or to Carians who had been invited to Athens ony for the time of the festival. The proverb is normally quoted as reading "Kares," but some sources add that there existed a variant reading "Keres": "as if the souls went through the city during the Anthesteria." It is hardly surprising that in the late nineteenth and early twentieth centuries when scholars saw souls of the dead everywhere the latter reading was pronounced to be the original one and the Keres interpreted as "souls of the dead," since a visit of ancestors had been abundantly demonstrated for "primitive" and Indo-European peoples.[122] More recently, however, it has been demonstrated that the reading "Kares" is certainly as old as "Keres," if not older, and there is now near unanimity that the evidence for a meaning "souls of the dead" for "Keres" is too slight to be accepted;[123] the mention of these souls may well have been caused by a misinterpretation of the word "Keres" by a later scholar. Despite this philological objection, some scholars still try to save the interpretation of "souls of the dead" for "Keres."[124]

[122] O. Crusius, in *Allgemeine Encyclopädie der Wissenschaften und Künste in alphabetischer Folge*, 2nd sec., vol. 35 (Leipzig 1884) 265-267; Rohde, *Psyche* 1. 239 n. 2; J. G. Frazer, *The Scapegoat*, 3rd ed. (London 1913) 152f.; J. Harrison, *Prolegomena to the Study of Greek Religion*, 3rd ed. (Cambridge 1922) 34-36, 42-49; L. Malten, *RE* suppl. 4 (1924) 883-900. L. Farnell, *The Cults of the Greek States*, vol. 5 (Oxford 1909) 221 n. b even accused the few scholars who still preferred the reading Kares of ignorance of anthropology.

[123] R. Ganszyniec, "Θύραζε Κᾶρες," *Eranos* 45 (1947) 100-113; M.H.A.L. van der Valk, "Θύραζε Κᾶρες or Κῆρες," *Revue des études grecques* 76 (1963) 418-420; J. Brunel, "Cariens ou Κῆρες aux Anthestéries: le problème philologique," *Revue philologique* 41 (1967) 98-104; A. Pickard-Cambridge, *The Dramatic Festivals of Athens*, 2nd ed., rev. by J. Gould and D. Lewis (Oxford 1968) 14; Burkert, *Homo necans*, 251; F. Graf, *Gnomon* 51 (1979) 213 n. 22.

[124] Burkert, *Homo necans*, 250-255 has taken a different direction and, accepting the antiquity of both readings, has tried to reconcile them by

It has been argued that the Greeks, being not as courteous as the Slavs who treated the returning souls well, applied the word "Keres," or "demons of death," to the souls, but this solution is hardly convincing.[125] Neither is the suggestion that the Keres are the destructive spirits of the crops and fields; there is no evidence to support this contention, just as there is no evidence that the Keres were spooks.[126] No convincing arguments, therefore, have hitherto been adduced in support of a connection of the Keres with the souls of the dead.

Much more convincing is Burkert's discussion of the ancient explanations of the reading Kares. The first explanation—the Carians were slaves who feasted and did not work—must derive, Burkert argues, from the circumstance that slaves were allowed to join in the drinking and feasting on the Choes. The other explanation runs as follows: "Once the Carians were masters of a part of Attica and when the Athenians celebrated the Anthesteria, they concluded a treaty with them and received them into the city and their homes. When after the festival some Carians were left behind in Athens, whoever met them said jokingly: "Out of the door

---

suggesting that the Keres, or "spooks" and Kares or "primeval inhabitants" are in fact identical but were called Kares in Attica. The difference would have been caused by an old declension *Kēr, *Kāros, which developed differently in various dialects: in Attica it became Kares, in Ionia Keres. However, it seems that this ingenious solution of an old declension can be rejected on linguistic grounds, and our sources give no support for a dialectic variation, see R.S.P. Beekes, "Κῆρες, Κᾶρες: root nouns of the type *Cēr, *Caros?" *Münchener Studien zur Sprachwissenschaft*, no. 36, 1977, 5-8.

[125] Against Nilsson, *Geschichte*, 225; see Pickard-Cambridge, *Dramatic Festivals*, 15 n. 1.

[126] J. ter Vrugt-Lenz, *Mnemosyne* 4, no. 15 (1962) 238 (destructive spirits); Burkert, *Homo necans*, 252 (spooks) who here follows U. von Wilamowitz-Moellendorff, *Der Glaube der Hellenen*, vol. 1 (Berlin 1931) 272, but who, however, in my opinion does not produce convincing evidence to prove his interpretation.

you· Kares ['Carians'], the Anthesteria are over" (Zenobius 4.33).

Burkert compares this explanation with a report of the Anthesteria in Marseilles.[127] On that day the gates were closed and the city acted as if it were at war. This was because, it was said, a few years after the foundation of the city the Ligurian king Comanus wanted to surprise the city on the Anthesteria by smuggling into it soldiers on wagons—probably the wagons with the casks of new wine as Burkert persuasively suggests—which were entering the city on that day. The conspiracy was detected because a Ligurian girl told the plan to her Greek lover and the invaders were caught and killed, as were the king and seven thousand of his men (Justinus 43.4.6).

Both explanations of the customs during the Anthesteria show a structural resemblance. On a certain day strange men, the primeval inhabitants, are allowed to enter the city. When their time is over, they have to leave again. This belief finds it proper place, as Burkert has seen, in the customs associated with the wearing of masks as it could still be observed in this century in remote valleys of the Swiss Alps, where at certain times of the year—usually around the New Year—masked men would enter the houses and request to be entertained, a request that could not be refused. Here, too, though, Burkert tries to harmonize "Kares" and "Keres" by explaining that the respect shown to the intruders derived from the idea that the intruders are the ancestors or former inhabitants of the country.[128]

---

[127] Also see J. Brunel, "D'Athènes à Marseilles," *Revue des études anciennes* 69 (1967) 15-30.

[128] The explanation of Kares as ancestors, which evidently derives from Meuli, *Gesammelte Schriften*, 1: 184, is untenable, since Meuli derived the "beggars' processions" (*Bettelumzüge*), which usually took place around Christmas and Shrove Tuesday, from similar behavior after the death of

A different approach seems preferable. Mourning periods as well as the periods marking the transition from the old to the new year and from abundance to Lent are liminal periods, periods between an old situation and a new one. One of the characteristics of these periods is a reversal of status; prominence is given to people who, in normal circumstances, fall into the interstices of social structures, live at the margin of society, or are looked upon as the scum of the earth, as Victor Turner has shown in a number of studies.[129] This prominence will have been the reason for the "Carian" explanation, since the Kares lived, according to the legend, at the margin of Athenian society. During the Anthesteria, though, they were allowed into the city in order to play their special role at the festival. Besides the visits of these marginals, the liminal periods also know the intrusion of supernatural beings, like the *manes* during the Roman Lemuria, the elves on May Day, or the witches during Walpurgis night;[130] the Keres as demons of death fit into these times as well. For this reason the Keres do not need to be identified with the souls of the dead; from a structural point of view Kares, Keres, elves, and witches are all representatives of a demonic, nonsocial, and unstructured world who

important people among "primitive" peoples. Here is one of those typical reductionist assumptions that can occasionally be found in the work of Meuli, whose whole scientific opus circled round the customs associated with the deaths of men and animals. The weak point is that Meuli's explanation does not make clear how and why this transference from a mourning custom to a calendrical rite occurred, and why the transference did not go the other way around.

[129] See especially the following studies: *The Forest of Symbols* (London 1967) 93-111; *The Ritual Process* (London 1969); *Dramas, Fields and Metaphors* (Ithaca and London 1974); "Process, System and Symbol: New Anthropological Synthesis," *Daedalus* 1977, no. 3, 61-80; *Process, Performance and Pilgrimage* (New Delhi 1979).

[130] Ovid *Fasti* 5.433; J. G. Frazer, *The Magic Art*, 3rd ed. (London 1912) 53 and *The Scapegoat*, 159ff.

117

are absent in normal times.[131] Although the historical relation between the readings "Kares" and "Keres" remains uncertain, they are structurally equivalent in this particular case, since both are entities that are normally absent from the world of the free Athenians.

When the normal structure of society is broken up, the situation becomes potentially dangerous, and people begin to feel insecure. This accounts for the special behavior in Marseilles during the Anthesteria. The festival's aetiological legend and the ritual have a striking parallel in modern Swiss tradition that seems not to have yet been noticed. In a number of Swiss cities it was related that long ago the city was almost surprised by soldiers whom the enemy tried to smuggle into the city in casks or barrels. Fortunately, they were detected by children or by a stroke of luck and the attack was foiled. Since then the night watchman has to go around on that particular evening with his familiar warnings, and a special cry connected with the detection of the enemy. These "murdernights" (*Mordnächte*) were all supposed to have happened—and consequently were remembered—on days in typically liminal periods such as the days in the middle of November, around Christmas, or Shrove Tuesday.[132] The seemingly ancient legends were obviously reinforced by the fact that these liminal periods in the calendar were indeed often occasions for revolution and rebellion.[133]

---

[131] This has been overlooked by Versnel, "Destruction, *Devotio* and Despair," 589 n. 206 who insists on the identity of the Keres with the souls of the dead.

[132] L. Tobler, *Kleine Schriften zur Volks- und Sprachkunde* (Frauenfeld 1897) 79-105 ("Die Mordnächte und ihre Gedenktage"); see also L. Zehnder, *Volkskundliches in der älteren schweizerischen Chronistik* (Basel 1976) 301f.

[133] This particular theme has often been studied by the maverick Swiss historian H. G. Wackernagel, *Altes Volkstum der Schweiz* (Basel 1956)

So, with Burkert we see in the "Carian" reading of the proverb a reflection of a custom in which persons who are perhaps masked enter the houses and ask to be feasted. The proverbial application of the saying to obtrusive people can be best accounted for by this explanation. Finally, it should be noted that this explanation presupposes the entering of real people, whereas Rohde and other scholars still thought of imaginary visitors.[134] It is unknown when the saying was

---

passim. Hans Georg Wackernagel (1895-1967), son of the great philologist Jacob Wackernagel, grandson of the well-known Germanic scholar Wilhelm Wackernagel, a friend of the late Karl Meuli (see F. Jung in Meuli, *Gesammelte Schriften*, 2: 1164, 1201 n. 3), collected in *Altes Volkstum* most of his studies on ancient Swiss history. These are of great importance for the history of the relation between festival and revolution, and for the history of the place of the young men in society, but during his lifetime they did not gain him the recognition he deserved, and they are unduly neglected in present discussions. A full bibliography of Wackernagel's writings has been published by T. Bühler, *Basler Zeitschrift für Geschichte und Altertumskunde* 68 (1968) 237-245. In this context I would like to thank Dr. iur. W. Wackernagel for information about his father. For festivals and rebellion in Switzerland, also see the following studies by P. Weidkuhn: "Ideologiekritisches zum Streit zwischen Fasnacht und Protestantismus in Basel," *Schweizerisches Archiv für Volkskunde* 65 (1969) 36-74; "Fastnacht-Revolte-Revolution," *Zeitschrift für Religions- und Geistesgeschichte* 21 (1969) 189-206; "Carnival in Basle," *Cultures* 3 (1976) 29-53.

Recently we have had the brilliant analysis of the bloody carnival of Romans by E. Le Roy Ladurie, *Le Carnaval de Romans* (Paris 1979), English ed. *Carnival in Romans*, trans. M. Feeney, (New York 1980). For France, also see N. Z. Davis, *Society and Culture in Early Modern France* (London 1975) 152-187; R. Pillorget, *Les mouvements insurrectionnels en Provence* (Paris 1975); D. Fabre, "La fête éclatée," *L'Arc* 1976, no. 65, 68-75; Y.-M. Bercé, *Fête et révolte* (Paris 1976). For revolution and rebellion, and carnival symbolism, also see M. de Ferdinandy, "Carnival and Revolution," *Atlas* February, 1964, 98-104; Davis, *Society and Culture*, 124-151 ("Women on top"), reprinted in B. A. Babcock (ed.), *The Reversible World* (London 1978) 147-190; P. Burke, *Popular Culture in Early Modern Europe* (London 1978) 199-205.

[134] Rohde, *Psyche*, 1: 239f.; Meuli, *Gesammelte Schriften*, 1: 222; Parke, *Festivals*, 116.

pronounced during the festival, but it may well have been after the drinking bout was over, for after the match the jugs and the symposium wreaths were brought to Dionysos' sanctuary. Aristophanes' Frogs (211-19) went "rambling in drunken revelry," and their behavior may well have been typical for the average Athenian. It had been a happy day, and it must have been happy memories that made Themistocles celebrate the Choes in exile, just as the Athenian Pollis did not forget the festival in faraway Egypt, and the philosopher Xenocrates showed his prowess in drinking at the Choes at the Sicilian court of Dionysius.[135]

The return to the normal structure of society took place on the last day of the festival called Chytroi, or "Pots," from the *panspermia*, a dish consisting of all kinds of grain, boiled in an earthen pot and sweetened with honey.[136] It was the major food of the Choes, and in keeping with the character of that day it was not prepared in the customary way; it made no use of the normal cooking techniques of milling and baking.[137] During the Chytroi the celebrants remem-

[135] For Themistocles, see Possis *FGrH* 480 F 1. For Pollis, see Callimachus fragment 178 Pfeiffer; see R. Scodel, *ZPE* 39 (1980) 37-40; J. Zetzel, *ZPE* 42 (1981) 31-33. For Xenokrates, see Diogenes Laertius 4.8; it is tempting to think that this Sicilian drinking bout was organized for, or perhaps by, Plato during his stay at Dionysius' court. This "happy" evidence has been insufficiently taken into account by those scholars who believe in a return of the dead during the Anthesteria. For example, Versnel, "Destruction, *Devotio* and Despair," 590f. tells us that the dead "were regaled in awe and terror," but this is pure fiction; our sources say nothing of the sort. Neither do we know that in Athens the deluge (below) was connected with "the unspeakable crimes of murder and cannibalism"; the Athenian Flood legend is virtually unknown. M. P. Nilsson, *Eranos* 15 (1915) 182, reprinted in his *Opuscula*, vol. 1 (Lund 1951) 147, already warned against these somber pictures.

[136] The *hieros gamos*, which was probably celebrated at the end of the Choes, may have been another sign of the return to the normal social order, see Versnel, "Destruction, *Devotio* and Despair," 589, 591.

[137] A similar technological regression took place in Eretria during the Thesmophoria, when the women did not fry the meat but dried it in the sun; the Thesmophoria were also a festival that changed the normal cul-

bered the survivors of the mythological Flood as having eaten this special dish as their first food. It is noteworthy that the survivors were not supposed to have eaten their food prepared in the normal Greek manner—similarly, the survivors of the Flood in Argos ate wild pears—but in a more primitive way: the transition from the chaos of the Flood into an ordered society had to happen gradually, as so often in important transitions.[138]

The Flood was associated with the social chaos of the Choes on the mythological level, and the restoration of the social order on the Chytroi is therefore appropriately connected with the survivors of the Flood.[139] In Greece, as elsewhere, the Flood was often thought to have preceded the origin or foundation of important constituents of the cosmic and social order, such as the course of the sun, sacrifice, the founding of a city, and, interesting in connection with our festival, even the mixing of wine: one of the inventors of mixed wine was Amphictyon, the son of Deucalion.[140] The emergence of an ordered society also expressed itself in the celebration of games on this day; similarly, in aristocratic milieus mourning periods came to an end with games—like the funerary games for Patroclus—in which the males once again could demonstrate their prowess and skill after a period of inactivity.[141] In the games

tural order, see Plutarch *Moralia* 298 C; Graf, *Eleusis*, 179; Burkert, *Griechische Religion*, 365-370; M. Detienne and J.-P. Vernant, *La cuisine du sacrifice en pays grec* (Paris 1979) 183-214.

[138] See Bremmer, in Vermaseren (ed.), *Studies in Hellenistic Religions*, 9-22. For Argos, see Plutarch *Moralia* 303 A; Aelian *Varia Historia* 3.39; Scholia on Euripides *Orestes* 932.

[139] Burkert, *Homo necans*, 265f.; Versnel, "Destruction, *Devotio* and Despair," 591.

[140] Burkert, *Homo necans*, index s.v. *Sintflut*; G. Piccaluga, *Lykaon* (Rome 1968) 69-75; F. Graf, *Museum Helveticum* 36 (1979) 19.

[141] Burkert, *Homo necans*, 266 compares the games after sacrifices, which seems less appropriate in this case. For funeral games, see now L. E. Roller, "Funeral Games in Greek Literature, Art and Life," (Diss. Univ. of

on the Chytroi the young men played an important role, as was suitable; the new order was exemplified by the prominence of the new generation. Not only the new generation of males was active, though; the maidens too had their festival, the Aiora, and the connection of the feast with the general theme of the Anthesteria was illustrated by one of the aetiological myths of that festival telling of the horrors of drinking unmixed wine.[142]

There is one other festival that should be mentioned in connection with the theme of the return of the dead. In Thessaly the main festival was called Peloria, which was characterized by great dinners, temporary freeing of prisoners, the invitation of strangers, and a status reversal of masters and slaves; like the Anthesteria, this festival was also connected with a Flood legend.[143] Meuli has connected the name of the festival, Peloria, with the adjective *pelōrios*,

---

Pennsylvania 1977) and "Funeral Games in Greek Art," *American Journal of Archaeology* 85 (1981) 107-119.

[142] Burkert, *Homo necans*, 266-269; J. Hani, "La fête athénienne de l'Aiora et le symbolisme de la balançoire," *Revue des études grecques* 91 (1978) 107-122; R. Scodel, *ZPE* 39 (1980) 37-40; S. Angiolillo, "La visita di Dioniso a Ikarios nella ceramica attica, *Dialoghi di Archeologia*, n.s. 3 (1981) 13-22.

[143] Herodotus 7.129; Baton *FGrH* 268 F 5; Nonnos *Dionysiaca* 6.373ff.; C. Sourvinou-Inwood, *Classical Quarterly* 24 (1974) 194f.; Meuli, *Gesammelte Schriften*, 1: 298f. and 2: 1041f. For similar classical "rites of reversal," see Bömer, *Untersuchungen über die Religion der Sklaven*, vol. 3 (Wiesbaden 1961) 173-195; H. Kenner, *Das Phänomen der verkehrten Welt in der griechisch-römischen Welt* (Klagenfurt 1970) 82-95, but both discussions are not entirely satisfactory. For the much better anthropological studies of this kind of rite, see the pioneering studies of Max Gluckman, *Custom and Conflict in Africa* (Oxford 1956) 109-136 and *Order and Rebellion in Tribal Africa* (London 1963) 110-136; P. L. van den Berghe, "Institutionalized Licence and Normative Stability," *Cahiers d'études africaines* 3 (1963) 413-423; E. Norbeck, "African Rituals of Conflict," *American Anthropologist* 65 (1963) 1254-1279; P. Weidkuhn, "The quest for legitimate rebellion," *Religion* 7 (1977) 167-188; Babcock (ed.), *The Reversible World*, passim.

meaning "monstrous, huge, terrible," and suggests that the etymology of the name points to the impressive ancestors; Nilsson, too, associated the name of the festival with the giants of the hoary past but these giants are not necessarily ancestors.[144] In the time of our source Baton, the third century B.C., the name was evidently connected with the epithet Pelor for Zeus,[145] and our source does not mention any visit by ancestors nor the wearing of masks which could be interpreted (as Meuli does) as ancestors. It is possible that in earlier times the Thessalians believed in a visit of the ancestors, but this has to remain a matter of conjecture. It seems certain that, so far, it has not been convincingly proved that the Greeks in historical times believed in a periodic return of the dead.

Conclusion

What was the early Greek concept of the soul of the dead? When we survey our material it is not difficult to draw a conclusion. The Greeks, like many other peoples, considered the soul of the dead to be a continuation of the free soul of the living. However, *psychē* was not the only manifestation of the deceased. The individual could also be represented as the body itself, as *eidōlon*, snake, and, perhaps, butterfly. In the transitional state between its stay in the body and in the afterlife the soul was thought to remain in the vicinity of the body where it is sometimes represented as a homunculus. As particularly indicated by the funeral rites of the period persons who died abnormally were considered to occupy an infranormal or supranormal status in

[144] Meuli, *Gesammelte Schriften*, 1: 298f., following Von der Mühll, *Ausgewählte kleine Schriften*, 436-441; Nilsson, *Griechische Feste*, 37.

[145] Pelor, and not the generally accepted Pelorios, will have been the original reading, see P. Maas, *Gnomon* 4 (1928) 571.

the life hereafter. Ghosts are as good as absent during the Archaic period and the saying "Out of the door, you Kares/ Keres, the Anthesteria are over" cannot be adduced as evidence for the return of the dead. Unfortunately, the fragmentary state of the sources does not yet allow us to establish the mutual relation of the manifestations of the deceased. Were there perhaps occasions on which the deceased was only represented as a snake or only as *eidōlon*? Here, there still remain questions that cannot as yet (if ever) be answered.

When we compare the soul of the living with the soul of the dead, we are struck by the negative way the souls of the dead are characterized. On the whole they are witless shades who lack precisely those qualities that make up an individual. This characterization corresponds with the type of society in which this particular collective attitude toward the dead developed. Homeric beliefs reflect the life of the small, closely knit communities of the Dark Ages where the life of the community was more important than the survival of the individual. In these communities death was not yet so much the end of one person's life but rather an episode in the history of the community and the life cycle. However, the sweeping changes in Greek society in the eighth century and after promoted an individualization that created individual concern for death and survival. In the new constellation the representation of the dead as witless shades lost much of its influence but it never disappeared completely.[146]

[146] For the important changes in the collective attitude toward the dead and death, see the highly stimulating study of C. Sourvinou-Inwood, "To die and enter the House of Hades: Homer, Before and After," in J. Whaley (ed.), *Mirrors of Mortality: Studies in the Social History of Death* (London 1981) 15-39.

Appendix One

The Soul of Plants and Animals

MODERN URBAN CULTURE has removed most of us so far from the world of nature that the attribution by many peoples of a soul to plants or animals comes as a surprise. Yet, in North Eurasia a few tribes ascribed a life soul to plants.[1] In Melanesia, as in North America, plants were even thought to have a free soul, although understandably there was no suggestion that plants could dream or swoon.[2] In the Archaic period such a belief is not explicitly mentioned, but Pythagoras thought that in the chain of reincarnations the *psychē* also entered plants.[3] The same belief was espoused by Empedocles who specifically forbade the chewing of laurel leaves, since he regarded the laurel as the highest form of plant incarnations, and even claimed to have been a bush himself in a previous existence.[4] A similar belief also existed among the Manichaeans, whose doctrines of metempsychosis had been influenced by Indian representations. The relevant evidence of Augustine, which once

[1] I. Paulson, *Die primitiven Seelenvorstellungen der nordeurasischen Völker* (Stockholm 1958) 123, 148, 161, 166.

[2] H. Fischer, *Studien über Seelenvorstellungen in Ozeanien* (Munich 1965) 267; Å. Hultkrantz, *Conceptions of the soul among North American Indians* (Stockholm 1953) 494f.

[3] Heraclides Ponticus fragment 89 Wehrli.

[4] Empedocles B 117, 127, 140 Diels/Kranz. For tree souls and plant souls in Greek mythology and paradoxography, see A. Henrichs, " 'Thou shalt not kill a Tree': Greek, Manichaean and Indian Tales," *Bulletin of the American Society of Papyrologists* 16 (1979) 85-108, esp. 85-92, 98.

used to be doubted, has now been confirmed by the newly discovered *Cologne Mani Codex*, in which a palm tree threatens revenge, and vegetables weep and cry with human voices.[5]

The documentation is much richer on a soul for animals. In Melanesia a free soul has been attributed to animals, although since this particular soul, like the soul of plants, was not mentioned as leaving the body during dreams, it must be only partially similar to the human free soul.[6] In North America there is a proper dualistic soul belief; in some areas the inhabitants have even thought that animals possess an ego soul. It remains obscure, however, exactly which animals are thought to have such a soul.[7] On this point our North Eurasian evidence is much more informative, since it appears that here domestic animals, especially the horse and the ox, were believed to possess a surviving free soul.[8]

A comparison of the animal soul with the human soul reveals that for the early Greeks the two souls had much in common, the main points of distinction being the absence of the *noos* and the absence of any mention of the *psychē* going to Hades.[9] Yet unlike the soul concept of other areas of the world, the Greek concept of the animal soul is noticeable for the near-absence of the free soul.

The *psychē* is mentioned only once in Homer. After Eumaios had killed a swine for Odysseus, "the *psychē* left it"

[5] Augustine *Contra Adimantum* 22, *De moribus Manichaeorum* 17.56; *Cologne Mani Codex* 6.1ff., 9.1ff.; L. Koenen, *Illinois Classical Studies* 3 (1978) 176ff.; Henrichs, " 'Thou shalt not kill a tree.' "

[6] Fischer, *Studien über Seelenvorstellungen*, 265-270.

[7] Hultkrantz, *Conceptions of the soul*, 495-501.

[8] I. Paulson, "Die Vorstellungen von den Seelen der Tiere bei den nordeurasischen Völkern," *Ethnos* 23 (1958) 127-157.

[9] See H. Rahn, "Tier und Mensch in der homerischen Auffassung der Wirklichkeit," *Paideuma* 5 (1953-54) 277-297, 431-480 and "Das Tier in der homerischen Dichtung," *Studium Generale* 20 (1967) 90-105; U. Dierauer, *Tier und Mensch im Denken der Antike* (Amsterdam 1976) 9 n. 21.

(14.426). However, no mention is made of this *psychē* going
to Hades. Since this was not always mentioned in the case
of the human *psychē* either, this absence does not necessarily indicate that the animal soul was not believed to go
to Hades; we just do not know. There are, though, reasons
to assume, as presented below, that the animal free soul
was not believed to go to Hades. After Homer, the only
animal that is said to possess a *psychē* in Archaic poetry is
the snake. Hesiod describes the sloughing of a snake's skin
with the words "Only the *psychē* remains," and Pindar mentions the *psychē* twice in the case of the death of a snake.
The attribution of a *psychē* to the snake may well have been
influenced by the snake's uncommon power of renewing
its skin.[10]

Many animals are said to possess a *thymos*. It is ascribed
to oxen (XIII.704; 3.455), swine (XII.150; XVII.22), horses
(XVI.468; XVII.451), wolves and lambs (XXII.263), a hare
(XVII.678), and a bird (XXIII.880). In the majority of these
cases the *thymos* is mentioned at the moment of dying, but
in such descriptions there is no differentiation between the
death of animals and the death of man. A *noos* is not ascribed
to animals. Only once is the verb *noein*, "to perceive," connected with an animal—when the dog Argus perceives
Odysseus (17.301)—but from this passage we can hardly
infer that animals were believed to possess a *noos*. A *menos*
is ascribed to a panther and a lion (XVII.20), a wild boar
(XVII.21), horses (XVII.451, 456, 476; XXIII.468), mules
(XVII.742) and an ox (3.450). Ego potencies were also ascribed to animals. Fawns (IV.245) and wolves (XVI.157) had

---

[10] Hesiod fragment 204.139 Merkelbach/West; Pindar *Olympia* 8.39,
Nemea 1.47; also see M. L. West, *Classical Quarterly* 11 (1961) 134-136;
W. Burkert, *Lore and Science in Ancient Pythagoreanism* (Cambridge,
Mass. 1972) 165; B. C. Claus, *Toward the Soul* (New Haven and London
1981) 63.

phrenes, and the lion an *ētor* (xx.169). Deer (i.225) and the lion (xx.169) had a *kradiē*, and horses (xxiii.284, 443) a *kēr*.

The near-absence of the animal free soul in early Greece has been explained by an indifference to the continued existence of animals after death.[11] Such an explanation does not, however, explain why the Greeks were indifferent in the first place. The reason for this lack of interest may well have been lack of a connection between hunting and the animal free soul such has been established for North Eurasia. The animal most often mentioned for that area as having a free soul is the bear.[12] It was the biggest game that hunters could hope for and around its killing an elaborate ritual developed, in which the hunters dissimulated their responsibility for the killing.[13] It was particularly important that the bones of the game remained undamaged, since the damage would reflect on the free soul of the animal. This care for the bones, and indirectly for the free soul, cannot be separated from the idea of the rebirth of the killed game.[14]

Among a number of peoples there exists a close connection between the animal free soul and a protector of all animals or sometimes those of a certain species. When the animal is killed, the free soul goes to the protector, who then insures the rebirth of the animal. The existence of the idea of such a protector, the Lord or Lady of the Animals, has

[11] Rahn, "Das Tier," 98f.; W. J. Verdenius, "Archaische denkpatronen 3," *Lampas* 5 (1972) 116 n. 23.

[12] See the exhaustive survey in H.-J. Paproth, *Studien über das Bärenzeremoniell*, vol. 1 (Uppsala 1976).

[13] K. Meuli, *Gesammelte Schriften*, 2 vols. (Basel and Stuttgart 1975) 2: 950-954; A. M. di Nola, *Antropologia religiosa* (Florence 1974) 201-262; A. Tanner, *Bringing Home Animals* (New York 1979) 136-181.

[14] See the detailed discussion by J. Henninger, "Neuere Forschungen zum Verbot des Knochenzerbrechens," in J. Szabadsalvi and Z. Ujváry (eds.), *Studia ethnographica et folkloristica in honorem Béla Gunda* (Debrecen 1971) 673-702.

been demonstrated for America, Africa, Asia, and the ancient Near East.[15] The idea was even alive until this century in Western Europe.[16] In ancient Greece Artemis had developed from such a Lady of the Animals.[17] As long as the hunting tribes kept their faith in the protector they were careful to avoid overkilling the game, since they believed they would incur the wrath of the god if they did not. Once missionaries or secularization eroded this faith the equilibrium between men and animals was disturbed, and the damage done affected both the animals and human society. This is illustrated in a fascinating study on the influence of

[15] For America, see Hultkrantz, *Conceptions of the soul*, 497-510 and in Å. Hultkrantz (ed.), *The Supernatural Owners of Nature* (Stockholm 1961) 53-64; J. Haekel, "Der 'Herr der Tiere' im Glauben der Indianer Mesoamerikas," *Mitteilungen Museum für Völkerkunde Hamburg* 25 (1959) 60-69; O. Zerries, "Wildgeister und Jagdritual in Zentralamerika," ibidem, 144-150 and *Wild- und Buschgeister in Südamerika* (Wiesbaden 1954). For Africa, see H. Baumann, "Afrikanische Wild- und Buschgeister," *Zeitschrift für Ethnologie* 70 (1938) 208-239. For Asia, see I. Paulson, *Schutzgeister und Gottheiten des Wildes (der Jagdtiere und Fische) in Nordeurasien* (Stockholm 1961). For the ancient Near East, see W. Déonna, "Daniel le 'Maître des Fauves,' " *Artibus Asiae* 12 (1949) 119-140, 347-374; W. Dostal, *Archiv für Völkerkunde* 12 (1957) 87-91 and "Über Jagdbrauchtum in Vorderasien," *Paideuma* 8 (1962) 85-97; M. Höfner, "Ta'lab un der 'Herr der Tiere' im antiken Südarabien," in *Al-Bahit. Festschrift Joseph Henninger* (St. Augustine 1976) 145-153. In Çatal Hüyük we already find a Lady of the Leopards in the sixth millennium B.C., see J. Mellaart, *Çatal Hüyük* (London 1967) pl. 9.

[16] See the important study by L. Röhrich, *Sage und Märchen* (Freiburg 1976) 142-195, 313-321; also see G. Eis, *Forschungen zur Fachprosa* (Bern and Munich 1971) 292-296; H. P. Pütz, "Der Wunderer und der Herr der Tiere," *Österreichische Zeitschrift für Volkskunde* 31 (1977) 100-115; M. Bertoletti, "Le ossa e la pelle dei buoi," *Quaderni storici* 14 (1979) 470-499.

[17] E. Spartz, "Das Wappenbild des Herrn und der Herrin der Tiere in der minoisch-mykenischen und frühgriechischen Kunst" (Diss. Univ. of Munich 1962); C. Christou, *Potnia Theron* (Thessaloniki 1968); W. Burkert, *Griechische Religion der archaischen und klassischen Epoche* (Stuttgart 1977) 267f. and, especially, *Structure and History in Greek Mythology and Ritual* (Los Angeles, Berkeley, and London 1979) 78-98, 176-187.

the fur trade on the Indians of Eastern Canada. Throughout this area widespread secularization occurred following white contact and the hunters started to kill the game indiscriminately, whereas before they often preferred to live on the brink of famine rather than to kill too many animals. Once the sanctions against overkilling were gone, the way was opened to a more convenient life style, but the consequences of this new way of living, alcoholism, and venereal diseases, exerted a devastating effect on the traditional Indian culture.[18]

Since hunters believed that the free soul returned to the protector of the animals, it is clear that the idea of an animal free soul functioned in a specific context, in a world where the rebirth of the killed game was anxiously expected. It may well be that here we find a key to the paucity of data about an animal free soul in ancient Greece. The Greeks were well aware that they were living in the era of agriculture and that they had left behind them the times when they had been hunters.[19] Consequently they may not have been particularly interested any longer in the continued existence of the animal free soul.

In post-Homeric times the doctrine of metempsychosis again ascribed a *psychē* to the animals and created the word *empsychon*, or "That in which there is a *psychē*," to denote living beings.[20] Empedocles considered that sacrificial slaughter was murder, and in his writings the human souls of the sacrificial victims protested against being killed,[21] but

---

[18] C. Martin, *Keepers of the Game* (Los Angeles, Berkeley, and London 1978).

[19] The change from hunt to agriculture is mentioned in a number of myths, see G. Piccaluga, *Minutal* (Rome 1974) 77-94; also see M. Detienne, *Dionysos mis à mort* (Paris 1977) 64-77.

[20] Burkert, *Griechische Religion*, 446, 448. The origin of this notion goes back at least till the time of Pythagoras, see Xenophanes B 7 Diels/Kranz.

[21] B 136f Diels/Kranz; see G. Zuntz, *Persephone* (Oxford 1971) 219-226.

Pythagoras, according to Iamblichus (*Life of Pythagoras* 85), denied a human soul to sacrificial animals. When Aristoxenos mentions that Pythagoras only refused to eat the ploughing ox and the ram, the implication seems to be that he ascribed a soul only to these animals.[22] Unfortunately, the fragmentary state of our sources does not permit an investigation of whether this is a revival of an older belief in which, as in North Eurasia, a free soul was ascribed to domestic animals.

[22] Aristoxenos fragment 29a Wehrli.

Appendix Two

The Wandering Soul in Western
European Folk Tradition

AN INVESTIGATION into Old Saxon and Old High German literature clearly shows that in the early Middle Ages the dualistic concept of the soul still existed in Western Europe.[1] This concept expressed itself in many versions of one type of folktale, in which the soul leaves the body in the shape of a small animal or homunculus and later returns to it. Versions of this tale have been recorded since the eighth century A.D. until modern times, especially from the more remote and rural areas of Western Europe. This strongly suggests that in these areas the dualistic concept of the soul continued to exist, whereas the cities and the élite had a unitary concept of the soul. I shall give two examples that are not mentioned in the authoritative survey of this type of folktale.[2] The Danish folklorist Feilberg has recorded the following story;[3] it is a good illustration of the motif involved and the themes that sometimes become attached to it.

Once, in the haytime, some people went to sleep in the afternoon

[1] G. Becker, *Geist und Seele im Altsächsischen und im Althochdeutschen* (Heidelberg 1964).

[2] See H. Lixfeld, "Die Guntramsage (AT 1645A)," *Fabula* 13 (1972) 60-107; also see V. Meyer-Matheis, *Die Vorstellung eines alter ego in Volkserzählungen* (Diss. Univ. of Freiburg 1973).

[3] H. F. Feilberg, *Sjaeletro* (Copenhagen 1914) 51f. For Feilberg, see B. G. Alver, "Henning Frederik Feilberg (1831-1921)," *Arv* 25-26 (1969-70) 225-238.

in a heap of grass. Among them was a girl who had a strange dream. At a short distance a man with a spade was grubbing about near a brook. Suddenly a tiny white mouse appeared which wanted to cross the little watercourse and was very distressed because it could not find a place to ford. When the man saw how confused the mouse was he laid his spade across the watercourse and the mouse forded it. He realised that he had never seen such a beautiful tiny mouse, so he followed and observed it. Near a big stone the mouse crept down and remained hidden for some time; it then returned and went back to the brook along the route it had come. The man put down the spade by which the mouse had crossed, and followed the mouse until it reached a heap of grass. There it vanished, but it seemed to the man that it had slipped into the mouth of the girl who lay sleeping there.

At the same moment the girl woke up and said: "Oh, what a strange dream I had. I thought I came into a forest which seemed to have no end until I reached a big river. I could not find a crossing but at last I came to a strange, peculiar bridge, the first part of which was made of iron and the rest of wood. Here I crossed safely and then I reached a big, grey stone castle which I entered through a very small door. There was no one to be seen, but gold and silver lay about in large amounts. After inspecting all the rooms I went back home and returned by the same bridge which now lay the other way round."

The man told the girl what he had seen and both agreed that the treasure must have some meaning. They lifted the stone and found so much silver and gold that they were never poor again.

This Danish folktale clearly shows how, during sleep, the soul represents its owner; the girl dreams what the mouse performs. It also shows two other motifs that frequently occur in this type of folktale: the crossing of water by the soul and the finding of treasure.[4]

---

[4] For the crossing of water, see M. Haavio, " 'A running stream they dare na cross,' " *Studia Fennica* 8 (1959) 125-142. For the bridge motif, see P. Dinzelbacher, *Die Jenseitsbrücke im Mittelalter* (Vienna 1973) esp. 127f. For treasure, see H. Fielhauer, *Sagengebundene Höhlennamen in Österreich*, Wissenschaftliche Beihefte zur Zeitschrift "Die Höhle" 12 (1969) 33-37 ("Die Schatz in der Höhle"); M. Eliade, *Zalmoxis, the Vanishing God* (Chicago 1972) 27-30.

The same motif occurs in a Dutch tale.[5]

Over a hundred years ago a farmer lived with his two daughters on a farmstead called Blijendaal, in the immediate neighborhood of St. Annaland. The girls were no beauties but a country lad from Brabant, Jan Marinusse, was courting one of the girls. One Saturday night about 8 o'clock he went to the farm to woo the girl. When they had been sitting for a while in a room the girl became so sleepy that the boy said "Just lean on my shoulder." So she did and soon she fell asleep. Suddenly he saw a bumble-bee creeping out of her mouth and flying away. He became worried and thought his girlfriend was a witch. He therefore took his handkerchief and spread it over her face. After she had been sleeping for twenty minutes the bee returned. The girl then became so short of breath that she got blue in the face, and the boy, afraid that she would suffocate, took the handkerchief off her face. Immediately the bee crept into her mouth, disappeared into her body, and she awoke.

The oldest example of this type of folktale occurs in Paul the Deacon's *History of the Lombards* (3.34), where the Frankish king Guntram has an experience very similar to that of the Danish girl; in Guntram's case the event is even supported by the "fact" that he donated to the grave of the martyr St. Marcellus a canopy adorned with precious gems from the discovered treasure. The literary form of the tale strongly suggests that the eighth-century historian adapted an oral version,[6] but this is naturally very difficult to prove. The authoritative survey of the tale found only a few medieval parallels, all of which were clearly inspired by Paul, as are many of the others that can be found in increasing numbers since the sixteenth century.[7] Yet, despite this result, it seems certain from a source that the authoritative

---

[5] J.R.W. Sinninghe and M. Sinninghe, *Zeeuwsch Sagenboek* (Zutphen, Holland 1933) 118f. I have quoted only the first part of the tale as Jan's further adventures are not relevant here.

[6] So Lixfeld, "Die Guntramsage," 86.

[7] Lixfeld, ibidem, 65ff.

survey did not consider that oral versions were widely current in the Middle Ages.

Oral traditions are on the whole ignored by medieval sources. It is only very recently that medievalists have started to interest themselves in the oral culture of the nonliterate classes. By using hagiographical sources, *exempla*, and records of the Inquisition, imaginative historians are increasingly successful in lifting at least a tip of the veil that covers the world of the subordinate classes.[8] The most successful of these recent investigations centers on Vatican records for the village of Montaillou in the Pyrenees where the Inquisition interrogated all the inhabitants in its crusade against the Cathars around 1300. In these records we find an oral version with anonymous characters and without discovery of the treasure.[9] The occurrence of the tale in such a remote part of Western Europe suggests that oral versions must have been much more widespread than our written sources would lead us to believe. Admittedly, this example does not constitute proof that Paul the Deacon did adapt an oral version, but it certainly shows that oral versions independent from Paul the Deacon's example were current during the Middle Ages.

In Western Europe, then, we can trace the endurance of the concept of the free soul. It may well be that we would have found the same in the more remote areas of ancient Greece, if only more sources had been available.

[8] See, e.g., J. Le Goff, *Pour un autre Moyen Age* (Paris 1977), English ed. *Time, Work and Culture in the Middle Ages* trans. A. Goldhammer (Chicago and London 1980); C. Ginzburg, *Il formaggio e i vermi* (Turin 1976), English ed., *The Cheese and the Worms*, trans. J. Tedeschi and A. Tedeschi (Baltimore and London 1980); J.-C. Schmitt, *Le Saint lévrier* (Paris 1979).

[9] E. Le Roy Ladurie, *Montaillou, village occitan de 1294 à 1324* (Paris 1975) 608, English ed., *Montaillou, the Promised Land of Error*, trans. B. Bray (New York 1978) 351f.

Selected Bibliography

Adkins, A.W.H. 1970. *From the Many to the One*. London.

Arbman, E. 1926. "Untersuchungen zur primitiven Seelenvorstellungen mit besonderer Rücksicht auf Indien, I" *Le Monde Oriental* 20, 85-222.

———. 1927, "Untersuchungen, II" *Le Monde Oriental* 21, 1-185.

———. 1963. *Ecstasy or Religious Trance*. Vol. 2. Stockholm.

Bérard, C. 1970. *L'Herôon à la porte de l'Ouest*. Bern.

Bickel, E. 1925. *Homerischer Seelenglaube*. Berlin.

Böhme, J. 1929. *Die Seele und das Ich im homerischen Epos*. Leipzig and Berlin.

Bolton, J.D.P. 1962. *Aristeas of Proconnesus*. Oxford.

Bömer, F. 1961. *Untersuchungen über die Religion der Sklaven in Griechenland und Rom*. Vol. 3. Abhandlungen der Akademie der Wissenschaften und der Literatur in Mainz, Geistes- und sozialwissenschaftliche Klasse 1961, no. 4. Wiesbaden.

———. 1963. *Untersuchungen*, Vol. 4. Abhandlungen 1963, no. 10. Wiesbaden.

Bremmer, J. 1979. "The Arrival of Cybele." In M. J. Vermaseren, ed., *Studies in Hellenistic Religions*, 9-22. Leiden.

Burkert, W. 1972a. *Lore and Science in Ancient Pythagoreanism*. Cambridge, Mass.

———. 1972b. *Homo necans*. RGVV, vol. 32. Berlin and New York.

———. 1977. *Griechische Religion der archaischen und klassischen Epoche*. Stuttgart etc.

———. 1980. "Neue Funde zur Orphik." *Informationen zum altsprachlichen Unterricht* (Steiermark, Austria) 2: 27-42.

Claus, B. C. 1981. *Toward the Soul*. New Haven and London.

Cole, S. 1980. "New Evidence for the Mysteries of Dionysos." *Greek, Roman and Byzantine Studies* 21: 223-238.

Darcus, S. M. 1979a. "A Person's Relation to ψυχή in Homer, Hesiod, and the Greek Lyric Poets." *Glotta* 57: 30-39.

———. 1979b. "A Person's Relation to φρήν in Homer, Hesiod and the Lyric Poets." *Glotta* 57: 159-173.

———. 1980a. "How a Person relates to θυμός in Homer." *Indogermanische Forschungen* 85.

———. 1980b. "How a Person relates to νόος in Hesiod and the Greek Lyric Poets." *Glotta* 58: 33-44.

———. 1981. "The Function of θυμός in Hesiod and the Greek Lyric Poets." *Glotta* 59: 147-155.

Detienne, M. 1977. *Dionysos mis à mort.* Paris.

Dodds, E. R. 1951. *The Greeks and the Irrational.* Berkeley and Los Angeles.

———. 1973. *The Ancient Concept of Progress.* Oxford.

Douglas, M. 1975. *Implicit Meanings.* London and Boston.

Dover, K. J. 1974. *Greek Popular Morality in the Time of Plato and Aristotle.* Oxford.

Eliade, M. 1964. *Shamanism.* London.

———. 1972. *Zalmoxis, the Vanishing God.* Chicago.

Felten, W. 1975. *Attische Unterweltsdarstellungen des VI. und V. Jh. v. Chr.* Munich.

Fischer, H. 1965. *Studien über Seelenvorstellungen in Ozeanien.* Munich.

Frazer, J. G. 1913. *The Scapegoat,* 3rd ed. London.

Gottschalk, H. B. 1980. *Heraclides of Pontus.* Oxford.

Graf, F. 1974. *Eleusis und die orphische Dichtung Athens in vorhellenistischer Zeit. RGVV,* vol. 33. Berlin and New York.

———. 1980. "Milch, Honig und Wein." In G. Piccaluga, ed., *Perennitas. Studi in onore di Angelo Brelich,* 209-221. Rome.

———. 1983. *Nordionische Kulte.* Rome.

Haavio, M. 1959. " 'A running stream they dare na cross.' " *Studia Fennica* 8: 125-142.

Harrison, E. L. 1960. "Notes on Homeric Psychology." *Phoenix* 14: 63-80.

Henrichs, A. 1979. " 'Thou shalt not kill a tree': Greek, Manichaean and Indian Tales." *Bulletin of the American Society of Papyrologists* 16: 85-108.

———. 1982. "Changing Dionysiac Identities." In B. F. Meyer, ed., *Self-Definition in the Greco-Roman World.* London.

Herter, H. 1975. *Kleine Schriften.* Munich.

Hertz, R. 1960. *Death and the Right Hand.* London.

Hultkrantz, Å. 1953. *Conceptions of the soul among North American Indians.* Stockholm.

Jarkho, V. N. 1968. "Zum Menschenbild der nachhomerischen Dichtung." *Philologus* 112: 147-172.

Kessels, A. 1978. *Studies on the Dream in Greek literature.* 2nd ed. Utrecht.

Kurtz, D. C. and Boardman, J. 1971. *Greek Burial Customs.* London.

Láng, J. 1973. "The Concept of Psyche." *Acta ethnographica academiae scientiae Hungaricae* 22: 171-197.

Lattimore, R. 1962. *Themes in Greek and Latin Epitaphs.* 2nd ed. Urbana.

Lixfeld, H. 1972. "Die Guntramsage (AT 1645A)." *Fabula* 13: 60-107.

Lloyd-Jones, H. 1971. *The Justice of Zeus.* Berkeley, Los Angeles, and London.

Mannhardt, W. 1884. *Mythologische Forschungen.* Strassburg.

Meuli, K. 1975. *Gesammelte Schriften*, 2 vols. Basel and Stuttgart.

Meyer-Matheis, V. 1973. *Die Vorstellung eines alter ego in Volkserzählungen.* Dissertation, University of Freiburg.

Mühll, P.v.d. 1975. *Ausgewählte kleine Schriften.* Basel.

Nilsson, M. P. 1906. *Griechische Feste.* Berlin.

―――. 1967. *Geschichte der griechischen Religion.* 3rd ed. Vol. 1. Munich.

Nock, A. D. 1972. *Essays on Religion and the Ancient World,* ed. Z. Stewart. 2 vols. Oxford.

Onians, R. B. 1954. *The Origins of European Thought,* 2nd ed. Cambridge.

Oppenheim, A. L. 1956. *The Interpretation of Dreams in the Ancient Near East. Transactions of the American Philosophical Society,* vol. 46, no. 3. Philadelphia.

Otto, W. F. 1923. *Die Manen oder von den Urformen des Totenglaubens.* Berlin.

Parke, H. W. 1977. *Festivals of the Athenians.* London.

Parker, R. 1983. *Miasma.* Oxford.

Paulson, I. 1958. *Die primitiven Seelenvorstellungen der nordeurasischen Völker.* Stockholm.

Peuckert, W. 1960. *Verborgenes Niedersachsen.* Göttingen.

Rahn, H. 1967. "Das Tier in der homerischen Dichtung." *Studium Generale* 20: 90-105.

Rohde, E. 1898. *Psyche*. 2nd ed. 2 vols. Freiburg and Berlin. English ed., *Psyche*, trans. H. B. Willis, London 1925 (quoted from the German edition).

Schnaufer, A. 1970. *Frühgriechischer Totenglaube*. Hildesheim and New York.

Schwidetzky, I. 1966. "Sonderbestattungen und ihre paläodemographische Bedeutung." *Homo* 16: 230-247.

Snell, B. 1975. *Die Entdeckung des Geistes*, 4th ed. Göttingen. English ed., *The Discovery of the Mind*, trans. T. G. Rosenmeyer, Oxford 1953 (quoted from the German edition).

Staehler, K. P. 1967. *Grab und Psyche des Patroklos*. Münster.

Sydow, C.W.v. 1948. *Selected Papers on Folklore*. Copenhagen.

Thomas, K. 1973. *Religion and the Decline of Magic*, 2nd ed. Harmondsworth.

Turner, V. 1969. *The Ritual Process*. London.

———. 1974. *Dramas, Fields and Metaphors*. Ithaca and London.

Verdenius, W. J. 1970. "Archaische denkpatronen 2." *Lampas* 3: 98-113.

———. 1972. "Archaische denkpatronen 3." *Lampas* 5: 98-121.

Versnel, H. S. 1980. "Destruction, *Devotio* and Despair in a Situation of Anomy: the Mourning for Germanicus in Triple Perspective." In G. Piccaluga, ed., *Perennitas. Studi in onore di Angelo Brelich*, 541-618. Rome.

Wackernagel, H. G. 1956. *Altes Volkstum der Schweiz*. Basel.

Wagenvoort, H. 1966. *Inspiratie door bijen in de droom*. Mededelingen der Koninklijke Nederlandse Akademie van Wetenschappen, Afdeling Letterkunde, Nieuwe Reeks, vol. 29, no. 8. Amsterdam.

Widengren, G. 1969. *Religionsphänomenologie*. Berlin.

Zuntz, G. 1971. *Persephone*. Oxford.

Index of Passages

Achilles Tatius, 5.16: 90; 7.13: 43

Aelian, *De Natura Animalium*, 1.51: 80; 10.21: 107; *Varia Historia*, 2.26: 33; 2.38: 110; 3.37: 104; 3.39: 121; 4.7: 91; 8.18: 107

Aeschines, 3.244: 96; 3.252: 91

Aeschylus, *Eumenides*, 103: 83; 104: 51; *Psychagogoi, Papyri Köln* 3.125: 77

Alcaeus ed. Voigt, fr. 38: 90

Alkimos *FGrH* 560, F 2: 110

Andocides, *On the Mysteries*, 137f: 90

Apollonius, *Mirabilia*, 3:26, 38; 4: 46; 6: 33

Apuleius, *Metamorphoses*, 8.8: 84

Archilochus, *Fragmenta*, 9-13: 90

Aristophanes, *Frogs*, 190f: 100; 211-219: 120; *Fragmenta*, fr. 222: 84

Aristotle, *Athenaioon Politeia*, 1: 91; *Historia Animalium*, 551 A: 82; *Metaphysics*, 984 B: 40; *Fragmenta*, fr. 61: 40; fr. 611, 28: 97; fr. 611, 29: 104

Aristoxenos ed. Wehrli, fr. 29a: 131

Arrian, *Epicteti Dissertationes*, 2.1.15: 102; 3.22.106: 102; 4.7.31: 92

Artemidorus, 2.9: 106; 4.4: 43

Athenaeus, 10.429 A: 110

Augustine, *Contra Adimantum*, 22: 126; *De Civitate Dei*, 18.18: 32; *De Moribus Manichaeorum*, 17.56: 126

Baton *FGrH* 268, F 5: 122

Bion ed. Kindstrand, F 70: 90

Callimachus, I.13: 43; *Fragmenta*, fr. 98: 107; fr. 99: 107; fr. 178: 111, 120

Cicero, *Tusculanae Disputationes*, 1.104: 92

Clearchus ed. Wehrli, fr. 7: 50

Cologne Mani Codex, 6.1ff: 126; 9.1ff: 126; 54.1: 38

Conon *FGrH* 26, F 1 18:34

Democritus ed. Diels/Kranz 68, B 166: 79

Demosthenes, 43.58: 99

Dio Chrysostomus, 5.17: 102; 31.85: 90; 66.20: 102; 73.7: 90

Diodorus Siculus, 3.33.5: 103; 16.25.2: 91; 18.47.3: 91; 18.67.6: 90

Diogenes, *Epistulae*, 25: 92

Diogenes Laertius, 1.35: 41; 4.8: 120; 6.79: 92; 8.20: 86; 8.21: 85

General Index

INDEX

Welwei, K. W., 99
Wendland, V., 87
West, M. L., 42, 84, 102, 105, 127
Widengren, G., 8, 14, 38, 41, 50
Wiegelmann, G., 14
Wijsenbeek-Wijler, H., 49
Wikenhauser, A., 19
Wilamowitz-Moellendorff, U. v., 8, 50, 115
Wild, R. A., 107
Wilhelm, A., 84
Williams, F., 35
Wilson, B., 30
wine, 109-111, 121-122

witches, 117
Wolters, P., 45
women, exclusion of, 42-43

Xenokrates, 120

Yochelson, W., 35
Young, R. S., 97

Zehnder, L., 118
Zerries, O., 129
Zetzel, J., 120
Zimmerli, W., 46
Zoroaster, 37-38
Zuntz, G., 106, 130

MYTHOS: The Princeton/Bollingen Series in World Mythology

DATE DUE